A Circle for Sisters

Stories from the Inside Out

To Kim:
Thank you sissy for supporting me!
May this book bless you and the women
and girls in your life to live authentically!
XOXO
Tracey J Thompson
2021

Tracey Lanier Thompson
Deidra Bass
Joie Hill
Mary Adams

ISBN-13: 978-1-954609-18-1

For information regarding special discounts for bulk purchases, please contact the publisher: LaBoo Publishing Enterprise, LLC
staff@laboopublishing.com
www.laboopublishing.com

Scripture quotations marked (NIV) are taken from the Holy Bible, New International Version®, NIV®. Copyright © 1973, 1978, 1984, 2011 by Biblica, Inc.™ Used by permission of Zondervan. All rights reserved worldwide. www.zondervan.com

Scripture taken from the New King James Version®. Copyright © 1982 by Thomas Nelson. Used by permission. All rights reserved.

The Holy Bible, King James Version. Cambridge Edition: 1769; King James Bible Online, 2019. www.kingjamesbibleonline.org.

Photography by:
Chosen Media
http://www.chosenmedia.com

Table of Contents

Praise for
A Circle for Sisters: Stories from the Inside Out

"Start Living Your Authentic Life"

"I think this chapter will have an infectious impact on women who are struggling to cherish and discover their authentic selves. You have specifically pointed out what steps and the procedure to remain 'true' to oneself using definitions and examples from your own experiences.

"I love what you said, that 'you deserve to be happy now, not just in a memory!' With all life's chaos, so many women get caught up in all the social roles we feel we have to play and what is so-called expected behavior as a mother, caregiver, wife etc... that we lose our joy and reflect on what happiness used to feel like when we had fewer responsibilities and did not have so many roles to play. We get complacent and stuck in the 'people pleasing mode' you spoke of. So true!"

Keisha Swanston
Educator, Cousin, Wife, Mother

"Authenticity resonated with me mostly because it truly is the path to freedom and peace of mind in life. I love how you gave many examples of your experience with being authentic and examples the reader can add to their life to strengthen theirs."

Kinshasa Jani
Author, Business Owner, Beautifull Soul

"I enjoyed reading your chapter, "Start Living Your Authentic Life." It was relatable and informational. If this was a separate writing on its own, I would buy it. Something that really resonated with me was truly the word 'boundaries.' Setting and creating boundaries are necessary to maintain an authentic/happy life. Knowing who you are, what you like and don't, and what you want and don't want."

Kimberly Bryant
Educator, Wife, Mother

"The Social Butterfly and Her Sisterhood Journey: Sisterhood Should be Sisterly"

"I really enjoyed reading about your relationship with your mother, grandmothers, and daughter."

Holly Biglow
Real-Estate Investor

"I personally am intrigued about your relationship with your mother, your older sister, and life at Western."

Vivian Adebyo
Mother, Life Coach

"Success is Never by Accident"

"I absolutely loved your chapter! It felt like a locomotive, chugging along at first. But then its fury was released! BAM, BAM, BAM, one explosive subject after another. What is the recipe for success? This chapter lays it out for me."

Venetta Jones
Entrepreneur, Wife, Mother

"A couple things stood out for me. Your "Why" making you cry. I never really thought about it like that! I guess your why is really what you are fighting for!"

Tracy Whitfield
Entrepreneur, Wife, Mother

"So many great nuggets, and I know so many aspiring entrepreneurs are going to be blessed by reading this. I really enjoyed reading your testimony and story, much of which I had no idea about. I loved the way you interlaced that with the mindset training and tips. Wow, bravo!"

Leslie Green
Author, Entrepreneur

Sisterhood

S is for the **STEPS** we take knowing we are not alone if we fall.

I is for the **INCREDIBLE** bonds that cannot be broken among true friends.

S is for **SOLIDARITY**—we stand stronger together.

T is for our **TRIBE** that always comes through with words of encouragement.

E is for being **ENCOURAGED** to cross the finish line and achieve our goals.

R is for the **REBELS** we are to tell our stories unapologetically and live our truths.

H is for **HILARIOUSLY** laughing with each other until our sides hurt and our eyes are teary.

O is for **OPENLY** accepting new queens into our circles.

O is for knowing it's **OKAY** to be yourself, to be accepted; don't change for anyone.

D is for **DEEPLY** loving our friendships and holding them near to our hearts.

SISTERHOOD is like a warm embrace
and is always there when needed.

– Mary Adams

Acknowledgements

Tracey Lanier Thompson

A special acknowledgement to my daddy, Clarence E. Lanier, who passed away on the evening of our first edits of this manuscript. He will never get the opportunity to read this book, but I thank him for being my first love and being the one who taught me to love myself first and how to receive and give love!

Thank you, Mommy, Catherine L. Lanier, for all the love and support you instilled in me, which gave me a foundation of positive self-esteem that allowed me to meet with great successes throughout life. I love you both beyond words!

To my husband, Mike (Ferg54), thank you for always supporting me and allowing me to shine and never asking me to dim my light for any reason. You have shown me the true meaning of agape love, the highest form of love; selfless, sacrificial, and unconditional love; persists no matter the circumstance.

To my children, Jabari Michael and Aliyah Laila, thank you for giving me my life's purpose—to give and receive love. You two are my heart walking around outside my body, my heartbeats. Being a mother is the best job I've ever had.

To my A Circle for Sisters sisters, Cover to Cover Book Club sisters, my tribe, and all my family and friends. For over twenty-five years I have lived my life's purpose and used my gifts to empower, strengthen, and uplift women. I want to thank everyone who has supported me personally or in an organized way. I want to thank anyone who has been there for the "strong" friend when I needed someone to lean on. Thank you; you are appreciated.

> *The meaning of life is to find your gift.*
> *The purpose of life is to give it away.*
> ~ Pablo Picasso

Joie Hill

Thank you, God, for saving me, keeping me, and ordering my steps.

I want to acknowledge my mother and my father. Her name was Janet Victoria Hill, and his name was James Marshall Hill. My mother instilled in me the character, morals, and values that have guided the way I live my life and how I treat people. My father worked hard, was a good provider, and a dedicated member of the Senior Male Usher Board at New Psalmist Baptist Church. He demonstrated a strong work ethic, saving money, and serving God. Both of my parents showed me love and the importance of family unity. Their spirit and legacy continue to inspire me.

To my baby girl, Jada Dachele. When you were a baby, I used to sing "You Are My Sunshine" to you. The words of the song are still true today and will always be true. I love you with every ounce of my being and more.

To all of my family and friends, thank you immensely for all of the love and support. There is no me without you.

To my dear Western, and especially the class of 1987 (Great Achievements and Success Make 87 Only the Best), thank you for traveling the journey of sisterhood with me. We have a bond and experience that only we as Westernites understand.

Deidra Bass

To God first and foremost, who created me and ordained me for his purpose long before I knew it. Thank you for keeping me, strengthening me, and never leaving or forsaking me.

To my husband, Kenneth Bass, who is my biggest champion, always letting me know that I can do all things through Christ who strengthens me and has encouraged me to step outside of man-made boundaries to be who God has created me to be. I love you, honey!

To my mom and dad. Mom, you taught me strength, independence, and sacrificial love. There's nothing you wouldn't do for your kids, grandkids, and family. Although you come across hard, you have the biggest heart. Dad, you always gave me unconditional love, and I'm still and always will be a daddy's girl. I miss you more than words can say. My heart still grieves that you're gone, but I'll forever cherish the memories—and your train rides to visit me. I love you both! Without you, there'd be no me.

To my kids, Kiarra, Andrea, and Andre Jr. My loves and my heartbeats! You bring so much joy and laughter into my life and the lives of others. You are truly some of the greatest human beings, and I'm super proud to be your mommy. Each of you are so different, unique, and spectacular in your own way. World, watch out for the imprint you're going to make on it! You'll forever be imprinted in my heart. I love you to infinity!

To my brother, Johnny, who introduced and opened my mind to entrepreneurship and being your own boss. You've always charted your own path. A natural leader. Thank you for setting the example, exposing me to more and not settling, and for being the best big brother ever! You've always protected me and had my back. I love you, bro!

To my tribe, my girlfriends, my sisters who hold it down for me, encourage me, and provide unwavering love and support and shoulders to cry and stand on, to laugh with until we cry and inspire each other. Your friendships have made this journey called life all the more sweet. I cherish and love you with my whole heart.

To all the people who have been bridges for me, especially my mentors Phyllis Wright and Chris Page. I appreciate you seeing potential and leadership in me long before I saw it in myself.

Mary Adams

To my daughter, Larissa, you have given me a purpose in life and a love like I have never known. Every sacrifice I have made has been for you and with you in mind. We stood against the most challenging times of our life together, side by side, hand in hand, and we survived, and we have a story that no matter how I try to put into words, no one will ever truly understand except you and me. Because of you, I had the courage to tell my story.

To my mother, thank you for every sacrifice you made and for loving me. You showed me what a strong work ethic looks like.

To my brother, Larry, whom I have always looked up to as my role model, even though you are younger. By example, you showed me how to go for my dreams and step out in faith, and trust that it will all work out. Thanks for always supporting me.

To all my friends and Cover to Cover Book Club members, thank you for all of the love and emotional support, and always being there whenever I needed encouragement, a shoulder to cry on, and for always refilling my wine glass.

To my fellow authors, we did it! This book project was our "baby" for the last year. We spent countless Saturday mornings and Wednesday nights on Zoom calls, time between writing our stories and researching how to get it published, etc., and now we have "birthed" our baby. Cannot wait for the next chapter!

Foreword

Women need stories. They connect us to one another and help us *all* learn and grow, for both the women who are sharing and the women who are bearing witness. This book was borne from the womb of women in circle—women reading and discussing stories together. Because they enjoyed the books and stories of other women, they continued to gather month after month and year after year. It was inevitable that they would share their own tales of struggle, celebration, and perseverance.

I'm so grateful they realized the ripple effect of story sharing. They are modeling, in their lives and in this book, how we all can normalize ongoing gatherings. Let this book be a testament to their journey and an inspiration to everyone who reads it. We need to tell our stories!

Amy R. Brooks
Author of *Stuff Your (Super) Mom Forgot to Tell You*

A note from the Editor -

Please express to the women who wrote this book how much I LOVED it! What a beautiful collection of stories and voices. It makes me want to be part of this collaboration! What I appreciate most is how honest every story is, the good, the bad, and the ugly. One thing that stood out is that maintaining relationships and friendships is hard work, even with family members (or maybe especially with family members), or just finding friends at the times when we need it the most. And then there are the personal, vulnerable moments that will really resonate with readers.

Alison - Senior Editor

Introduction

This book collaboration was started as a movement, *#TheBookTheRetreatTheMovement*, to collaborate on a book with ladies from my book club Cover to Cover Book Club, as well as ladies from my other organization A Circle for Sisters. The idea to do a book collaboration was born on an annual book club retreat to Deep Creek Lake, Maryland, in January 2020. On the retreat, as ladies do, we relaxed, had fun, and shared stories.

After we returned, I reached out to my dear friend, author, and book coach, Amy R. Brooks, for assistance in helping us work on a book collaboration. Several ladies were interested, but only a few were able to complete the collaboration of Volume I, which you are holding in your hands now. With this book, *A Circle for Sisters: Stories from the Inside Out, Vol. I*, we plan to start a MOVEMENT! We want women to use their voices to live, learn, grow, share, and most of all, HEAL!

Tracey Lanier Thompson

Start Living Your Authentic Life

Tracey Lanier Thompson

I praise You, for I am fearfully and wonderfully made.
Marvelous are Your works, and that my soul knows very well.
~ Psalm 139:14, NKJV

I chose to write this chapter to let women know that they don't need permission to live their authentic life. It's ironic that although I'm a seventies baby, I grew up with a very strong and independent self-image. I grew up during the era of *Leave it to Beaver*, *Happy Days*, and *The Brady Bunch*. The mothers, women, and girls in all of these shows appeared to be happy for the most part, but at times they struggled with feelings of independence and freedom when it came to household chores, school, dating, sports, or working outside the home (which didn't exist for the women and girls at that time on TV).

Even as a young girl in elementary school, because of my upbringing, something didn't feel right about this. In *Leave it to Beaver*, the mother, June Cleaver, stated in one episode, "Girls can become other things." I think she wanted to be more than just a housewife.

Carol Brady of *The Brady Bunch* had six children, so they gave her Alice the housekeeper. Carol wasn't allowed to work, but she still had the dream of working, so during reunion shows she was allowed to fulfill the dream of having a job outside the home. She became a real estate agent.

Marion Cunningham on *Happy Days* remained upbeat. She never had any problems. She had just "happy days." Even I knew this wasn't real!

The one show that came close to showing women in a realistic light was *Laverne & Shirley*. They were funny, quirky, and adventurous. They were single, had jobs, and seemed to be living their authentic lives. My parents probably didn't even know I was watching this show! I loved watching it with my older sister, Linda.

My household reflected some of the above characteristics in these sitcoms, but not all. I lived in the suburbs. My family moved to Northwest Baltimore County in 1971, when I was two years old, for my father's job. My mother was a stay-at-home mom. She walked me to the bus stop every morning and met the bus every afternoon. When I arrived home after school each day, I had an afternoon snack waiting, I did my homework like clockwork, I watched *Captain Chesapeake*, *The Flintstones*, *The Jetsons*, etc., and got ready for dinner to be served around five or six every evening. My mother cooked everything from scratch, including dessert. She made meals to order (if requested), which is why I'm a picky eater to this day (some say *spoiled*). She never said, "Eat what I fixed for dinner." It was, "What would you like for dinner?" My mother washed, ironed, folded, and put away everyone's clothes. You could say I lived inside one of the above sitcoms.

However, the big difference was the mindset and foundation that was instilled in me by both my mother and especially my father. Although my father was the provider and the protector, he never made any of us feel controlled, inadequate, or unworthy. He was the one in control of the finances. I can only speak from what I saw from my perspective as a child; my father provided everything we needed to build us up and to encourage us, not to make us feel indebted to or controlled by him, like some men do. Everything from the best clothing and shoes, taking us on the best vacations to the "Real Disneyland Park" in California several times, and Rocky Mountain (my fave). We had the *World Book Encyclopedias* and *The Child Craft Set: The How and Why Library* (a fifteen-volume set).

My father poured into the three women in his life to let them know they could be and do anything they wanted. He provided us with nice material things, but he also provided us with lasting memories of family vacations and family bonding time. Whether it was Sunday afternoons at Carvel on Reisterstown Road, getting my favorite vanilla ice cream cone with chocolate sprinkles, or taking the next flight to our next vacation, it meant we were going to spend time and have some fun. My father loved having fun and spreading it with the people around him.

Because of him, I knew I could do or be anything I wanted to be, and I belonged anywhere I wanted to be. Knowing that you belong is very important for a person's self-worth, for all women, especially women of color. It was important growing up during the seventies, where I was the only African American girl in my class from first through third grade, and I was often one of few African Americans in my college program at a small private college in Stevenson, Maryland, in the late eighties and early nineties. I continue to need this foundation of a positive sense of self-esteem as a Black woman.

As we know, diversity is often not reflected in society, so parents, please let your children know they are worthy, and they belong.

I spent every other Saturday of my childhood having "hair day" with my mother and sister. My mother spent those Saturdays shampooing, conditioning, braiding, straightening, perming, rolling, and curling our hair to perfection. These Saturdays were spent with my mother using her hands to bring us together, not just to do our hair and make us feel pretty, but also to create a special bond between us all. My mother setting aside this time to focus on us also contributed to my confidence and self-esteem. This time brought about countless conversations, laughs, and memories that I may not have appreciated at the time.

We spent time discussing fashion; my mother made all our clothes. My sister modeled my mother's signature fashions in all the high school fashion shows, and my friends remember my handmade fashions to this day. We discussed food; she cooked everything from scratch. We discussed family. My mother was the only one of her siblings to move from the south up north. We discussed friendships. With my mother being a stay-at-home mom, she was a mother to all the neighborhood children. All my friends loved her. They came to our house for meals, to get their hair done, and to have conversations.

During our Saturday morning hair days, we discussed anything going on in our lives. My mother carving out this undivided attention made me feel special and secure. It also instilled in me a sense of positive self-esteem, which led to confidence, leadership, and an ability to maintain healthy relationships because I never felt a sense of unworthiness or a need to compete, especially with women.

Along with my mother's nurturing spirit, my father provided a solid foundation for security and protection. He was a provider, and I was a true Daddy's Girl. My father was an original "Girl Dad." He worked a lot, but he always made time for me. He couldn't move without me by his side. I spent my time as a child with him, going on drives in his fancy, new, and always clean cars, going for lunch dates to McDonald's to get my favorite cheeseburger meal, hot fudge sundae, and apple pie, and riding on the back of his motorcycle through the back roads of our suburban neighborhood. My father always made me feel like a princess. Even after my parents' divorce when I was twelve years old, I still looked forward to the lunch dates and car rides.

> *A daughter needs a dad to be the standard*
> *against which she will judge all men.*
> ~ Gregory E. Lang

The attention, dedication, and nurturing that my parents put into raising me showed me a window into how I would treat myself, and an expectation for how I would allow others to treat me. The nurturing instilled in me a sense of self-worth. As I've gone through school, friendships, boyfriends, and now marriage and having children, I use all of the love and support instilled in me to create an authentic and happy life that works for me. Just maybe, what I share can help you do the same. However, even with a foundation of love and support, life will happen. It's up to you to remain true to your authentic self.

Staying true to your authentic self doesn't come overnight. It takes time, dedication, and a conscious effort to always seek truth, and that begins with the truth of who you are authentically.

Living an authentic life is an ongoing process of setting boundaries and routines that allow for your happiness and freedom. It's nice to have a partner you can delegate things to, but it truly never ends.

Although you can delegate—if you're like me and you have to make sure things are done, it can get tiring. Work, shopping, ironing, cooking, checking folders, emailing teachers, helping with homework and projects, date nights . . . the list goes on. Having babies fifteen months apart was no easy task. I had to learn early that my husband and children understood that I would not be the one turning into Momzilla. It wasn't easy, but I needed to continue a life pleasing not just to my family, but me too.

I needed to continue to practice self-care, sister circles, vacationing with the girls, and Lifetime movie marathons while maintaining the life of wifey and Mom Boss. But I wasn't willing to give *all* of myself in order to do so. I had always loved who I was and what I represented. I knew I deserved and needed to remain true to myself in order to be happy and authentically there for my family. I knew the journey to being my authentic self would never end. Having high self-esteem allows me to stay true to my authentic self.

Let me help you find or maintain your authentic self while being there for the ones you love.

In order to live an authentic life, you need three important things: **positive self-esteem**, a **decision** to be happy, and **connections** with the people and things you love.

Positive Self-Esteem

Being true to your authentic self means that what you say aligns with your actions. It is who you are to your core. It's about being true to yourself through your thoughts, words, and actions. When we aren't in touch with our authentic self, it's easy to go into people-pleasing mode and do and say things based on what is expected of us or based on social and peer pressure.

Being true to your authentic self isn't easy. In today's society with social media, people share beautiful ideas, pictures of new homes, vacations, and all the great things their children are doing. All of these things often may be an editing of their authentic lives. We tend to live our life based on obligations, expectations, and "shoulds." This can prevent us from being true to our authentic self and living in the now. Some of the risks to being true to your authentic self include people not liking you and your decisions, people judging you, and having your feelings hurt.

However, the benefits greatly outweigh the risks. The benefits of being your authentic self are living in the now, doing things that make you happy, and following your passion regardless of who you disappoint or how it may be perceived by others. Everyone won't respond well to your authentic self because of how it may impact them.

When living authentically, we are being vulnerable and giving others the opportunity to love us and accept us for who we are. We are showing the good with the bad. This allows for more intimate and honest relationships and unconditional love.

Maintaining positive self-esteem is a continuous journey throughout life. It starts with parents nurturing their children and making them feel worthy. Then, it continues with setting standards based on your needs and upholding those standards. Checking in with your inner self will help you maintain positive self-esteem. Periodically, ask yourself, *How am I feeling? What's working? What's not working? What am I proud of?* Answering these questions will help you take a pause and reflect, reevaluate, and refine your life, which leads to living an authentic life. Feeling like you have a good idea of what's working and what's not working gives you a sense of ownership over your life and will boost your self-esteem.

A Decision to be Happy

Making a decision to be happy is essential to living an authentic life. Happiness lies within the things that bring you joy. You must start with knowing what you like and don't like. You'd be surprised, but the average person may not be able to list things that authentically make them happy. When asked, they often associate happiness with their children, significant other, or not anything directly related to them at all. Often, this is because we don't get the opportunity or the time to do the things that make us happy. We do what our parents, teachers, or society says we should do and forget what truly makes us happy.

When asked what makes them happy, people often have to go back to childhood memories for reminders of happiness. That shouldn't be the case. We rarely stop to think about what would make us happy right now and take intentional steps to be happy. We feel we can't control our happiness; we're too old, don't have enough money, or have made too many bad decisions. However, knowing what you like and don't like will allow you to live an authentic life, where your actions are aligned with what you say and do. You deserve to be happy now, not just in a memory.

You know you are being authentic when your job gives you a sense of purpose and fulfillment rather than being drained and lacking energy; when your relationships are based on honesty and respect for who you are; and when you are able to present the real you in all situations rather than someone you are not. I'm very in tune with who I am, what I do and don't like, and what I want and don't want. Knowing these things about yourself allows you to be authentic or true to yourself and others. Once you get a handle on who you are authentically, you learn to protect and nurture who you are and set boundaries to maintain it and be happy.

You're only one decision away from being happy and living your authentic life.

My happy place is between the pages of a book or relaxing at the spa. I love pizza, Panera Bread, and Olive Garden (all pretty normal and reasonable things). I love buying school supplies, checking my children's homework folders, and helping with school projects. I love researching, acquiring knowledge and information, organizing things, meeting new people, and having lunch with friends. I love all things women and girls, and creating spaces for positivity.

I don't like cooking, clutter, adults who lack personality, small talk, or pumping gas. I don't like sand at the beach, outside sports, or grocery or clothes shopping.

Not being afraid to let the ones around me know my likes and dislikes allows me to live in the now and be happy. When I'm feeling overwhelmed with life, my family already knows where they can find me and what things make me happy. No one feels slighted when I let them know I'll be at my biweekly standing manicure and pedicure appointment on any given Saturday. No one feels jealous when I let them know that I'm going to brunch with my bestie or leaving for my bi-monthly book club discussion, girls-only vacation, or annual book club getaway.

For two weeks, follow these simple steps to being more authentic:

Simple Steps to Being More Authentic

1. Take a break from social media to allow yourself to focus on you and not others' "edited" versions of life.

2. Think about what you are doing versus what you want to be doing (in a day, week, month, year, life). Take the time to reflect and ask yourself why you are doing certain things and not doing other things. Are you doing things based on obligation, or based on how others will respond?

3. Take out a pen and paper. Journal and track how you feel when you are more authentic versus when you are not feeling your authentic self. Are these changes physical or emotional? Do you feel happy, guilty, or tired when you are not authentic? Does your breathing or appetite change? Do you get headaches? Are your thoughts more positive, negative? Are you more or less focused?

4. Volunteer. Find an issue you care about or that you were always curious about but never pursued. This may bring you closer to your purpose and living authentically.

5. Take mental health breaks, away from your work or other priorities, to take care of you. This may mean a fifteen-minute reset in the middle of the workday, or it may mean taking a day off once a quarter in order to better handle the upcoming weeks.

6. Educate yourself on mental health and wellness. Learning about mental illness, its symptoms, and how it affects your life can help you address any challenges you may experience while on the journey to living your authentic life.

7. Share your story. One of the best ways to live your authentic life is to share your own personal experience. If you're considering sharing your story, remember that you have control over what pieces you share. The goal of sharing your story is freedom, and to help other people know they aren't the only ones going through something and that there is hope. Remember, your story may be your own, but it's not for you.

The goal of being 100 percent authentic to yourself is to remember that the journey never ends. It will not happen overnight. Continue to check in and ask yourself if your thoughts and feelings match your behaviors; this is where true authenticity lies.

Establishing self-care practices is crucial to maintaining your authentic self and being there for your family. There are different types of self-care: emotional, physical, social, practical, mental, and spiritual. When I'm overwhelmed with work, family, mommy-ing, and wife-ing, I escape to one of my happy places or do something I love. On a Saturday, between dance and basketball, you won't find me grocery shopping. You will find me meeting a girlfriend for lunch or stealing away to Barnes & Noble (without guilt). My family needs groceries, but I'm running the children to activities, so I delegate the trip to the market to my husband (without guilt).

If you don't have a partner, develop relationships with fellow parents or family who can help you steal away for a few moments of sanity. I've been spoiled by my mother and sister; they both assisted with my physical self-care for years. As I mentioned, my mother practiced self-care with my sister and me every other Saturday growing up with our hair days. Hair days fulfilled more than one category of self-care. They provided physical, emotional, and spiritual self-care.

By the time I got to high school, my sister had become a cosmetologist and continued the rituals of self-care. She took it a step further by providing the full beauty salon experience—hair, manicures, pedicures, massages, the works. All of this led me to implement these self-care rituals into my life throughout college, marriage, and children. No one and nothing stands between me and my standing self-care appointments. The same applies to the gym, although, it's a ritual I enjoy sharing with my family, especially once my children were old enough to go to the gym and work out with me.

Throughout the years, I found that if my emotional, physical, mental health, etc., aren't being maintained, I create what I need to feel fulfilled and aligned with my authentic self. The outcomes have been to create the A Circle for Sisters organization and the Cover to Cover Book Club. These two groups have been going on for over twenty years. These two favorite things were created out of my need for self-care and the need to live authentically and to be happy.

Having these outlets allowed me to stay connected to two things I love: reading and sisterhood.

Get to know who you are and what you want, and if you don't currently have it in your life, create it—for your happiness. Once you've tapped into your authentic self, who you are at the core, knowing your wants and needs, as well as what you don't want and need in your life, you work on ways to maintain this in your life.

Authenticity is a collection of choices that we have to make every day. It's about the choice to show up and be real. The choice to be honest. The choice to let our true selves be seen.
~ Brené Brown

Making a decision to be happy will help you maintain an authentic life. This will require setting boundaries. You need positive self-esteem in order to set boundaries. You must be confident and feel that you are worthy of living your authentic life to have others respect your boundaries and your authentic lifestyle. For me to be happy, I learned to create boundaries around my time and with people. Creating boundaries is a decision. It isn't an easy thing to do, but making conscious decisions can change your life.

As women, especially wives and mothers, we are taught to provide for, and be there for, everyone else, sometimes at the expense of our own needs and wants. We know there are innate differences between men and women, physically and emotionally. I don't think many will argue with the belief that women are the nurturers and are more emotional and communicative beings, while men are by nature the providers and fixers; and they are less communicative, especially when it comes to their emotions.

Because of these differences and beliefs, women often get the short end of the stick when it comes to marriage and parenting. They may suffer the weight of raising children and keeping marriages intact, no matter how they are equipped to handle parenting and marriage. Society seems to feel like just because you're born with breasts and a vagina and can give birth, you will automatically know how to be Mother of the Year, and in many cases, the badass or Lady Boss in the boardroom, and continue to look like the girlfriend at home!

The only way to face this Superwoman façade is to set boundaries in all areas of your life. This means at home, at work, and with your family and friends. Be warned that people may not like your boundary setting, especially your family. However, it's a mandatory step in staying true to your authentic self. In order to stay true to yourself, you need room to explore who you are and to continually maintain and grow in your happiness.

Not being true to your authentic self manifests in many different ways: health issues such as obesity, migraines, high blood pressure, and fatigue. The emotional problems can include being short-tempered, argumentative, having low self-esteem, and a lack of focus and attention. Taking control of your authentic self by setting boundaries allows you to be more productive, happier, and more accessible to the ones who need you and love you.

Setting healthy boundaries allows us to maintain authentic relationships.

I can remember coming home from the hospital with my son, my firstborn. After reading many parenting books and magazines regarding how life will change with a newborn, I took everything with a grain of salt—so as to not get overwhelmed with all the information—and decided to use some of the information along with some good old common sense. I also listened to my pre-mother voice in my head, as well as my mother's words of wisdom.

As I mentioned earlier, I already maintained self-care as an important aspect of my life. Taking care of myself first—which is not selfish—allows me to be a happier, more fulfilled person, which in turn allows me to be there for those around me without regret or animosity.

So, as I brought my beautiful baby boy home, I knew I had to figure out how to maintain my standing mani-pedi appointments, hair appointments, Thursday date nights with my husband, book club, sister circles, my Lifetime movie addiction, and all the other things that make me authentically happy. In the back of my mind, I could hear my mother's words of advice that have stuck with me throughout my parenting and marriage: "You don't let the children rule the house."

At that moment, as I recalled those words, I knew things were going to be okay because this parenting thing was going to be done on my terms, not an infant, toddler, or adolescent's terms. My mother also said, "Let the baby cry sometimes; don't pick him up constantly. He needs to learn to soothe himself."

She told me not to worry about having noise around him. Some people with babies are constantly telling you, "Shush, the baby is sleeping!" My mother told me if you have to vacuum and the baby is asleep, then vacuum, and he will get used to it. She said don't worry about him being in a swing. If you need to clean, cook, or whatever, do it, and put him in the swing, walker, or highchair.

So, as I started the parenting thing, I set boundaries that pertained to both my children and my husband. For me, this wasn't too hard, but it wasn't so easy either. Having a new baby enter the picture is a big adjustment to the parents' lives. When I had my son, we had only been married three years. We were getting adjusted to marriage and then had to make room for another whole person, who would be totally dependent on us. Although I had these preconceived notions of setting my boundaries and knowing what my authentic self needed as a mother—yes, we are the nurturers, most times, the one the baby cries for the most, and the one to get the job done. Therefore, I knew it was important that I put boundaries in place for my child(ren) and husband.

It started with nursing. Besides it being excruciatingly painful for me, I didn't appreciate the fact that I was the only one able to do this, especially at three in the morning. For the few weeks that I struggled to nurse my son, I would look over at my husband sleeping while I had to break my sleep and feed my son. I was the one who had to adjust my schedule or dismiss myself to go nurse during gatherings.

I understand the nutritional benefits and the bonding that takes place during nursing, but it put limitations on me that I started not to like. I projected these bad feelings toward my husband. I would be angry with him in the morning after not getting enough sleep due to nursing all night and morning. I was upset because he didn't have to hook himself to a machine and pump before leaving the house.

I stopped nursing for two reasons: one, it was painful, and two, I felt restricted, and I needed my freedom back. The same freedom my husband had. I realized (without guilt) that my son would get nurtured and the nutrition he needed from me holding a bottle and feeding him. Plus, my husband needed to take part in these middle-of-the-night feedings. More balance was needed in order for me to remain true to my authentic self, even during feedings.

I communicated my feelings of overwhelm and being restricted surrounding nursing to my husband. He wanted to be involved with my son however he could and for me to be happy, so we moved on to bottles and life was good for all. I made a decision. My life was changed for the better, and I was happy.

Even my newborn son had to learn boundaries! As my son learned to sleep through the night, I could hear my mother's words regarding him needing to learn to soothe himself. After bathing, feeding, and cuddling, I put him in his crib, and my infant son had to learn to soothe himself. We both learned that if he began to whimper or cry, eventually he would soothe himself and fall off to sleep without Mommy coming to rescue him throughout the night.

This gave me freedom to cook, clean, watch TV, talk on the phone, read a book, or be with my husband. I was not going to let my child run the house or cause me to lose my authentic self in the abyss of parenting. And little did we know that he needed to learn to soothe himself because when he was just seven months old, I found out his sister was on the way!

I also had to set boundaries with my husband. Once I was no longer connected to my son by the breast, I felt like I needed to let my husband know that not only could he take part in the feedings, but he would be equally involved in every aspect of our parenting experience. Fortunately, through six months of premarital counseling, we discussed roles in marriage, in which we decided there are no roles, per se. We have certain beliefs based on the foundation of what marriage means to us in our faith, but as far as roles, whoever does something best, then that is your job or contribution to the marriage. We needed to take this belief into our parenting as well.

Setting boundaries for your freedom, especially with the ones you love, doesn't just magically happen. You must be specific—and do it in love. As I said, we had our son three years into our marriage, so we were still in our honeymoon phase and still enjoying a lot of our time together and with our friends. Before having my son, I still attended my book club and sister circles. My husband still spent time with his boys playing golf, basketball, coaching, and going to weekly happy hours. Initially, I felt obligated as a mother to put things off in order to take care of my son, but after realizing that I was the only one making adjustments to my outside activities, mainly due to the lack of energy and feeling overwhelmed, I decided I had to once again set some boundaries and routines in order to be happy and stay true to my authentic self.

When my son was seven months old, I found out I was pregnant with my daughter. I knew some things had to change.

My husband is awesome. He has always been the cook in the house, and he, like most husbands, will willingly do any tasks I ask him to do—cook, clean, grocery shop, get the dogs groomed, drop off and pick up. However, you get to a point where you're tired of delegating. You wonder if there will ever be a time when you will not think about everyone's schedules, the market list, shopping, what's for dinner (even though he will cook it), shopping for clothes and shoes, checking folders, school projects? Then you realize that time will never come! So you set routines and boundaries to help reduce the overwhelm, fatigue, and unhappiness.

Once my daughter was born, I had to sit my husband down and discuss the fact that there wasn't enough time for him to work, coach, and attend weekly happy hours. We had to set boundaries around our free time and time surrounding our family. Just because I enjoy being home on Friday (mainly because I'm exhausted after work, mommy-ing, and being wifey), that didn't mean he should leave me every Friday to go to happy hour while I entertained and took care of two babies. We had to set boundaries over our time and schedules that would allow us *both* to continue to do things that brought our family joy. I needed to be able to have free time, whether it was in the house or outside of the house. He needed to be there for that to happen. I set the boundaries over my home in order to remain true to my authentic self and to be happy.

As my children got older, I set boundaries and routines for them as well. My friends would call me and ask, "Where are the kids?" I let them know that they were either involved in activities or asleep. I put in the time and effort to put my children on schedules, which created boundaries that allowed for time and freedom and peace of mind. Setting boundaries around my time has allowed me to remain true to myself. I made sure that my schedule allowed for quality time with my children, and once they would go to sleep (at a set time every night), I had the freedom to be with my husband or do whatever I needed or wanted to do. I was happy.

Setting boundaries around my time wasn't the only thing I found I needed to do to remain true to my authentic self. In my opinion, it is hardest to set boundaries with people. Fortunately, most of my friendships have been long-lasting and true friendships. There were a few fair-weather friends along the way, but that's okay. Life is about change, and marriage and having children are some of the greatest changes a person goes through. Dealing with the changes affects you and the people around you.

I didn't have to set too many boundaries with people after getting married, but I found that once I had children, I did. I had to set boundaries with family members regarding my time and expectations surrounding my support—physical, emotional, and financial. I had to set boundaries that emphasized the importance of prioritizing my time and energy around my husband, children, and the things that make me happy. I had to put my family first (without guilt). It was hard for some people, especially family, to adjust to taking a different place in my life.

Once you set boundaries with time and people, believe it or not, you will have more of yourself to give. The people around you will adjust to your boundaries, and they will appreciate the opportunities you share with them. Although setting boundaries may be difficult for you and the people around you, setting them can make you a happier person and allow you the time and freedom to live an authentic life.

Connections

Having high self-esteem and putting boundaries in place has allowed me to be happy. Because I'm confident in who I am and what I want and deserve in life, I have the time and freedom to stay connected to the people and things I love. Connecting to the things and people you love is another important aspect to living an authentic life. All my career choices have been based on the impact I want to have in the world and the people I will be connected with. Living an authentic life provides me with the opportunity to do this.

After college, I started working in the legal field in an area of law that didn't align with my ideals. I wasn't happy. Initially, I decided to work there because of the money and prestige. However, I found myself with people and working under conditions that didn't align with my beliefs. The employer didn't fit with my values regarding family and other things. My job wasn't allowing for the true connections I wanted in my life.

Therefore, in order for me to stay true to myself, I chose to leave that place of employment. I had enough confidence and self-worth to know that I didn't have to stay in a job I didn't feel connected to.

Even within my career, I feel the need to connect with my authentic self. There are a few reasons I chose to be an educator, but the main reason was that it was a more meaningful and fulfilling career. I love making connections with children, all types of learners, and serving. Education allowed me to surround myself with interactions where I was able to grow and serve. I was living authentically. I was happy. Through my career connection, I was doing something that made me happy. Not many people can say that about their jobs/careers. However, if you are living authentically, even your career can be aligned with who you are authentically.

Staying connected to your authentic self in social interactions is important too. There's a saying by Jim Rohn: "You are the average of the five people you spend the most time with." This statement resonates with me because I choose to make connections with people who are positive and contribute to my life, rather than bring negativity and drain my life. Making a conscious decision to be connected with people and opportunities that are aligned with your authentic self is important in order to be happy.

I spend time in church, masterminds, book clubs, serving on commissions, and with true friends. Connections that make me a better person.

Making decisions to be happy in my career that align with my authentic self has allowed me the opportunity to make more meaningful connections outside of my career as well. I'm able to spend more quality time with my family and serve in the community. If I didn't think about remaining true to myself and the connections that I make, I wouldn't be able to teach vacation Bible school, serve on my city's Women's Commission, volunteer for eleven years as my daughter's Girl Scout troop leader, or serve for seventeen years on both of my children's parent associations.

If I didn't make conscious decisions to connect with the things I love, I wouldn't have the time for standing Thursday date nights with my husband or Sunday dinners with a core group of family and friends, or even to take part in this book collaboration. All of these connections align with me authentically, and it's important for me to remain connected to them in order to be happy.

I surround myself with authentic and loving people who share my journey of personal growth and awareness.

Most importantly, living authentically has allowed me to connect with my husband and children in a meaningful way. This is the most important connection of all. Having the confidence to make decisions in my personal life and career has allowed me the time and freedom to be there for myself and my family without guilt. Knowing that my actions are aligned with what is best for me and my family provides me with a sense of happiness. My living an authentic life has served as an example to my children, as well as my husband and the people around me.

Both of my children will know they are loved and worthy to be loved. My daughter will know she is worthy and allowed to be happy. Whether single or married, she will know she doesn't need permission to put herself first and make decisions that make her happy, without guilt. I have taught her this is not selfish, it's self-love—staying true to yourself and living authentically. She will know that if she stays true to herself, everything else will fall into place in life.

My son will know that his wife is an individual before she is his wife or the mother to his children. He will know to encourage and support her efforts at home and outside the home. He will nurture her self-esteem instead of feeling threatened or trying to tear her down.

Living an authentic life has helped my husband encourage and support me. It hasn't been all peaches and cream. We have had to maintain open and honest communication throughout the different stages of our marriage along with an authentic and agape love for each other. That's another story altogether. I will leave you with a quote from Eckert Tolle: "Only the truth of who you are, if realized, will set you free."

Authentic Testimonies from the Ones I Love

Jabari Thompson

Living your authentic life has motivated me to continue to grow and live my own authentic life. You spoke to me about your goals and what you wanted to do. Yes, it was communicated with love! Of course we've had tough conversations about our future as a family, yet we've always communicated with love and good intentions.

My mother balanced motherhood, wifehood, and womanhood so beautifully. She took time for herself when needed, and maintained her routines that made her happy while also adding me and my sister, Aliyah, to some of them to share her joy. My sister and I enjoyed just sitting in the nail salon listening to music and talking to our Auntie Wa, listening to her talk about her day and the funniest things that happened at work, to her making my favorite meal, fettuccine alfredo. If anybody is a superwoman, it's my mom.

• • •

Aliyah Thompson

You lived an authentic life by doing and creating anything you wanted to. Always being yourself and not caring about what others think about your journey in life. Even if people overlooked what you were doing, you still put your all into anything and everything, for your own sake, and knew that at least you felt and knew that you succeeded. You've communicated this to me by showing me that any task I want to finish or want to fulfil, no matter how hard or tiring it may be, can be completed. That showed me that if you can get things done, I can too.

The way you live your authentic life is definitely communicated with love. You always make sure everyone else is okay, physically and mentally, even before you make sure you're okay, from you being Life Coach Tracey to managing a book club, to your A Circle for Sistas—now A Circle for Sisters—groups. You have always humbly cared for and expressed love to many people involved, and even uninvolved, in your authentic life.

I don't think we've had to compromise anything individually or as a family for you to live your authentic life. If you want something, you make sure the family is good before you start another endeavor. You have never left us hanging because you wanted to focus on something individually. I feel that you living your authentic life and pursuing what you want has definitely made you better as a person. It shows me and many others how to be the best we can be, go for whatever we want, and be about our business.

I think the best tools for a healthy family and household are honest and healthy conversations, and to have a checkup moment here and there. Like when we would do the dinner game, Roses and Thorns. We would go around the table and ask each person to share the rose (the best or most special part of their day) and the thorn (the most difficult part of their day). This was a way for us to share about our day or whatever was going on in our lives with each other.

You also always bought Jabari and me fun journals and devotionals to write in and express our feelings in case we had things we didn't want to share with you. It's important to occasionally talk about the positive things going on in life; maybe writing those thoughts down would help, as well as writing out the negative thoughts to get them off your chest. Just making sure everyone is living a peaceful and positive life.

• • •

Michael Thompson

Your authenticity has affected me in ways unimaginable. I've become more transparent to really understand who I am as a man and husband, along with my thinking process. During our marriage, however, it became more apparent that I was made to feel at ease and honest with having dialogues or simple conversations. In some situations, the communication became tense, but I learned to understand that the true nature of the communication was based on genuine caring and not hostility. I believe your authentic ways were always based on love because you've shown that you truly care about yourself, our children, others, and me.

I believe that your authentic personality challenged our marriage and had some compromising moments. There were times when I couldn't or simply did not want to accept many of your beliefs that were communicated, and they weren't comforting and were sometimes too authentic and transparent. Before negatively reacting to you, I learned to look at myself first and see how your authentic nature was affecting me, instead of taking out any negative emotions on you. This didn't happen early on in the marriage. It took time. Then, eventually, I learned not to see your social life as interference, but saw it as an outlet for you to do what you were passionate about, and live your authentic life.

Movement Step, Action Step

Commit to one action that you're going to take this month that moves you forward in a positive direction to living your authentic life. It can be taken from the section above, Simple Steps to Being More Authentic, or feel free to come up with your own. Be you. The world will adjust. Stay true to your authentic self.

The Social Butterfly and Her Sisterhood Journey:
Sisterhood Should Be Sisterly

Joie Hill

What is sisterhood?

When I think about the meaning of sisterhood, what immediately comes to mind is the phrase "I am my sister's keeper," which implies positivity and something that is good. I imagine a female who is supportive, loving, loyal, kind, considerate, and respectful toward other females, whether they are family, friends, coworkers, classmates—or even women they do not know at all because they are strangers whose paths have crossed.

As I see it, and as others have also said, sisterhood is a verb. It is demonstrated by the way females treat each other, regardless of whether they are acquainted. That treatment is partially guided by what is in the heart, what is in the mind, what is valued, and what is believed. It is also guided by personality, background, and life experience. Realizing that the way females treat each other is based on those factors and may vary, sisterhood can range from non-existent, to good, to bad, to downright ugly.

Sadly, women do not always have each other's backs. I am pointing out the negative and unhealthy truth of sisterhood not to pass judgement or attack, but to inspire and encourage positive and loving treatment among females of all ages. Life is a journey, and sisterhood is as well.

With that in mind, through personal experiences, witnessing the experiences of others, and observing what is shown through mass media, social media, and the world at large, a woman can see and apply the lessons learned on the right way to treat other women. I have hope for those who are still learning and those who may not even realize the blessings of showing love to fellow women. In a perfect world and in my dreams, all females would embrace the spirit of "I am my sister's keeper" and adopt it as a lifestyle.

> *Sisterhood is about showing up, and standing up,*
> *and loving, and giving, and teaching, and being a*
> *cheerleader and champion.*
> ~ Megan Minutillo

Dancing with Sisterhood

I believe we are born with a spirit and a soul. Along with our spirit and soul, I feel that a major aspect of our personality is born naturally. I am convinced that I marched into this world as a true people person. I attribute that to my deep love for people, and because I am talkative. I am known for striking up conversations with just about anybody, anywhere. For instance, I met a young lady a few years ago while shopping at the Coach store. She was an associate, and our conversation started with me asking her about a purse she was carrying. She has a Caribbean accent and I inquired where she was from. After learning her background and why she was in Baltimore, we became friends on Facebook. Since she only has a few family members in the United States, I told her I would be her aunt. I call her Niece instead of using her real name.

Over the years, we have kept in touch, and she has a piece of my heart. She is now expecting twin boys, and I am excited to have two nephews on the way.

In another situation, I met a friend who I call my big sister in an AOL chat room for African American women around 1998. The group met periodically, and we connected outside of the group. We shared information about ourselves and our families. We even exchanged holiday gifts. Life happened, and we did not keep in touch as much. However, we reconnected during the pandemic and continue to talk as if no time ever passed.

It has always been easy for me to meet and interact with others. My spirit is fed, nurtured, and filled through my connections and relationships. If interacting with people were a place, I would always be found there.

I treasure creating good memories and when I reflect on them, my heart dances and sings. I especially value spending time establishing, cultivating, and maintaining relationships with women. My unequivocal, absolute truth is that I need women in my life to survive. When I reflect on the years from my childhood to now, I have met and interacted with women in my family, where I lived, attended school, worked, introduced through others, or randomly encountered just by being out and about.

I am fifty-one years old now, and many of them are still traveling with me on this incomparable journey called life. Along the way, I have experienced the gifts of joy and love—as well as the agony of pain and disappointment—in sisterhood. My sister friends showed up and showered me with much love at my fiftieth, all-female birthday party. Turning fifty was a milestone that I struggled with deeply, because it was a wake-up call that I had probably already lived the bulk of my life and it represented the next chapter, identified as middle age. I thought often about my future and what I wanted to experience and accomplish. Those thoughts were stressful, scary, and included developing a will and facing my mortality.

As if that were not enough, I was on the rollercoaster ride of being menopausal and having a hard time with sleep disturbances, hot flashes, and dry skin. I once had a hot flash that was so intense, I had to leave a book club meeting because I became weak, felt like I was going to faint, my stomach was queasy, and I had to use the bathroom. However, having my sister friends celebrate me made all of that a little easier to embrace because most of them had already turned fifty and were welcoming me into the club.

I also had the enormous pleasure of celebrating for an entire year by going to several fiftieth birthday parties, taking an epic trip to Jamaica with forty of my high school classmates, and attending a semi-formal group birthday party that was a night to remember, filled with dancing, eating, laughter, and lots of picture taking.

On the flip side, sisterhood has not always been pretty. I have experienced some disappointments and pain in my friendships, like the time I was not invited to a gathering with friends and saw the pictures afterward on Facebook. Or the time I had plans with a friend to take a trip abroad that I was very excited about and then she canceled. I am sure that along the way, I, too, have unintentionally done or said things that were hurtful, and I apologize to anyone I have offended and ask for forgiveness.

Those emotional highs and lows are all part of being human. Between our attitudes, values, beliefs, backgrounds, dreams, fears, communication styles, and personalities, we are some complex creatures. That explains why being in female relationships can be both rewarding and challenging for us all.

Despite everything I have been through, it has been for my own good. I wholeheartedly believe a part of my purpose is to encourage healing and to champion healthy and positive relationships among women.

Sisterhood is a journey. Not a destination.
-Author Unknown

About Me

My views of sisterhood were undoubtedly formed in childhood. When I was growing up during the seventies, I lived in the Baltimore neighborhood called Hilltop, in the northwest area of the city. When my family moved there, I was seven and already familiar with the street we lived on because one of my first friends lived there as well. We went to St. Ambrose Catholic School; she pretended to be my mom during recess and we rode the school bus together. (I still call her my "play mother.")

There were children in almost every household; in fact, there were very few people who did not have siblings, and there was a good mix of boys and girls of all ages. Children from nearby blocks hung out on mine and we did all the typical things children did during that time. We had the absolute best of times riding bikes, playing hide-and-go-seek, boys chase the girls, "Mother, May I," roller skating, dodgeball, four square, and skelly. I loved all of it and spent as much time as I could outside with my friends.

Living and growing up in Hilltop was a great experience for which I will always remain grateful because of all the good times shared with my friends and family. I tell people that I grew up in the best neighborhood in the world, and more than forty-five years later, I am still connected to people from Hilltop.

I remember being outside so much, especially during the summer. For some reason, my parents did not make my siblings and me come into the house when the streetlights came on—probably because the neighborhood was safe; a community in which neighbors knew and helped one another. I was even able to stay out later than some of my older friends. We used to tease each other by singing the Mickey Mouse Club theme song whenever someone had to go home. It was embarrassing for my friends to be serenaded while being escorted by one of their parents into the house. Fortunately, I never had the song sung to me.

I am the second of four children and have two sisters and a brother. My oldest sister, six years older than me, is an introvert. Unlike the rest of us, she stayed in the house most of the time and had a small circle of friends. Aside from them, she was also close to just a few family members. I vividly recall often being asked why my sister did not come outside. I realized that we were different, but of course did not have the wisdom to understand why. I was merely concerned with playing outside with my own friends.

I had even more friends in the Catholic elementary and middle schools I attended, where the rules were strict. That was hard for me, since I am a talker. Many a day I found myself getting demerits—sanctions for misconduct—for talking too much. Accumulating demerits led to punishments that ranged from detention to expulsion.

During recess, lunchtime, basketball practice, riding the bus, and on the phone, I constantly socialized with my school friends. One of my fondest memories from middle school was using the three-way phone feature for a conversation I orchestrated, with ten to fifteen teenagers laughing and talking over each other. It started off by calling one person with a three-way phone and telling them to call other people who had it too. Thank God my parents made the sacrifice for my older sister and me to have our own phone line in our room. I am guessing the monthly bill was between $30 and $40. At that time, having a three-way phone was a big deal, although I am certain they were desperately seeking peace of mind because of the constant bickering between the siblings to use the single phone line. And I will admit that I wanted to monopolize the phone.

As a teen, I had many friendships with girls, and there were several "besties" and crews along the way. Like most best girlfriends, we lived, loved, laughed, created memories, and shared precious moments together. Plus, we shared secrets and got into mischief, like knocking on elderly neighbors' doors and running. There were the occasional moments of not getting along, but we always seemed to work things out. It was during these moments that I learned, although I did not realize it then, just how valuable female relationships are.

I had a bestie that lived on my block. We were one year apart and were inseparable. One day, she invited me to go on the annual Hershey Park amusement park trip with people from her school. Back then, amusement park bus trips were major events, and I was looking forward to going. Of course, it was also another opportunity to interact with people. And the bonus would be connecting with people I felt I knew because of what she shared with me about them.

At the last minute, I was also invited to go to the Kings Dominion amusement park with my cousin. The thrill seeker and social butterfly in me did not want to miss out on having any amusement park fun. Since funds were limited, my mother told me I had to make a choice; there was no way I could do both. I decided to go with my cousin and had to tell my best friend. Of course, it did not go over well at all. She was disappointed and, expectedly, let me have it. Fortunately, we made up and moved on. In fact, we ended up going to Hershey Park the next year and had a great time.

When I revisit that situation, I am reminded of how easy it is to damage a relationship with female friends and just how important it is to keep promises with them.

Despite the friendships with classmates I had always enjoyed, in my last year of middle school, I vowed to myself that I was done with Catholic school. My mom really wanted me to go to a Catholic high school, but I was adamant about not going. My oldest sister graduated from a Catholic high school, and I guess my mom wanted the same for me, but I was beyond tired of wearing a uniform and operating under all the strict rules. It was time for a change.

Going to public school was appealing, and there were a lot more people to meet and befriend. Just about all my neighborhood friends attended public school and it seemed fun. My mom has since gone on to glory, and if she were still alive, I could not thank her enough for letting me apply to public school.

Of the three public schools I applied to, Western High School was my first choice. It was established in 1844 and is the oldest all-female public high school in the United States. The standard is excellence. Students are prepared and expected to achieve both academically and professionally. Good grades are required for admission and it is one of the best high schools in Baltimore City.

Western is a very special place that is rich in tradition, sisterhood, and the empowerment of young women to make their mark in the world. The school motto is "We have received light. Let us give light." The slogan is "Only the Best," and the school mascot is the dove. Students and alumnae are known for being smart, classy, and sophisticated, and Western girls were—and still are—identified as the cream of the crop. It is easy for alumnae to recognize each other, even when they are strangers.

Ms. Sandra Wighton was the principal when I was there. She epitomized grace, class, intelligence, confidence, professionalism, and style. A few notable graduates include former Baltimore Mayor Stephanie Rawlings Blake, author Harriett Cole, journalist Lisa Respers France, and actress Anna Deavere Smith.

I was extremely excited when I got accepted and was looking forward to going there in the fall all summer long. One summer evening, I attended a party at a recreation center and met a Western girl. I must have asked her a million questions over the loud music, all about her experience and what I could expect. Looking back, I am guessing she was annoyed with me because we spent more time talking than dancing.

When fall finally arrived, several of my middle school friends and a bestie from Hilltop began Western with me. There were other friends from Hilltop who joined me there later. All of it was a bonus.

I recall the nervous, excited energy I felt at freshman orientation, and distinctly remember my homeroom teacher and the details of meeting one classmate.

From the day of freshman orientation through graduation, I learned valuable lessons about sisterhood and friendship. There were a few thousand girls from all over Baltimore City, all with different personalities, interests, and backgrounds. As expected, I connected and became friends with many of them.

There was also a Big Sister, Little Sister program that paired incoming freshmen with juniors, to bond and get support adjusting to high school. I knew my big sister prior to arriving there because her father lived in Hilltop as well.

I was such a social butterfly, I even made friends with younger girls in the incoming classes. I met one of my dearest friends, whom I consider a sister, in the spring before she entered Western. We were at Rhythm Skate, the neighborhood skating rink, and I was wearing a gray leather miniskirt and a red leather jacket with three pleats in the front on each side. That night, I specifically told her I would see her when she got there. When she arrived that fall, I was a junior and we began a friendship that has lasted over thirty-five years.

I have another dear friend I also identify as a sister. We first met in the Western auditorium, and I asked her a million back-to-back questions without even giving her a chance to complete sentences. Another friend commented, "Dang, Joie, are you going to give her a chance to answer the questions?" (The three of us still laugh about that.) When I could not talk with her during class, I would write her notes. She has traveled through life with me for more than thirty-five years as well.

The adage that "birds of a feather flock together" was apparent at Western. Although the student body was racially, ethnically, and socio-economically diverse, girls who had something in common tended to find each other and connect. There were the exceptionally smart girls who were in the E course, completed ninth and tenth grades in one year, and then went to eleventh grade the next year. They hung out together.

Then there were the divas, some of whom were part of the Fashionettes, a competitive modeling club. They were close. The punk rockers dressed and wore their hair like members of punk rock bands; on the opposite side of the spectrum were the preppy girls, whose style was conservative, but not boring.

There were many other friendship circles, and sometimes a person floated between them and sometimes they did not. I was fortunate to have friends from elementary school, middle school, Hilltop, and new friends from all over Baltimore City there that I bonded with. Overall, there was appreciation and respect because we were all Westernites growing in sisterhood and developing friendships that have lasted for many years.

For me and my sister classmates, the Western slogan of "Only the Best" is an expression of not only our academic experience and how we govern ourselves in the world, but the relationships that were forged through those years.

Like most Western girls, I had the average, gut-wrenching teenage growing pains, coupled with the joy of love and support from family and friends. There were plenty of he-say-she-say issues, unspoken competitions, jealousies, and conflicts that usually involved a boy from the neighboring high school, Polytechnic Institute, or another school. With a building full of thousands of personalities going through puberty, there was certainly some drama.

Just about every boy I met had a personal history with another Western girl, and even without the benefit of social media, it did not take long to find out who she was. Obtaining details about her and then automatically disliking her, for no reason other than the fact that she was the ex-girlfriend, was the norm. Plenty of boys also dated two Western girls at the same time. As fate would have it, and/or because Baltimore is small, these triangles would soon be uncovered and would usually end with arguments, he-say-she-say issues, and girls not liking each other.

Although that teenage foolishness is laughable now, there was also, most importantly, plenty of sisterly bonding through the Big Sister, Little Sister program, spirit week, freshmen week, sophomore week, junior week, senior week, fundraisers, selecting class slogans, attending assemblies, hanging out on the outside courtyard (called the quad), riding the bus, numerous clubs, sports, parties in the cafeteria, preparing for proms, and gatherings outside of school. I have dear memories of going to a popular club called Odell's, going to basketball games, roller skating, double dating, and shopping with my friends.

One of the many rich traditions was students having their school ring turned on their finger the number of times that equates to the last two digits of their graduation year. Since I graduated in 1987, I had my ring turned eighty-six times, and documented each person who turned it! The last turn was reserved for the celebratory semi-formal ring dance, where the student's date would turn her ring under a decorated arch and then kiss her.

Some of the other activities I fondly remember include Spirit Week, the Spring Revel (which was similar to a carnival but on a smaller scale), the Sweetheart Dance for Valentine's Day, and the end-of-year Senior Banquet, where some seniors got awards based on votes for specific categories.

There are two school songs, and the one titled "Dear Western" is sung at almost every gathering. One of the most beautiful traditions is the format of the graduation. Graduates wear all-white gowns, carry single, long-stemmed red roses, and move in unison.

Another sisterhood activity at Western is the annual Unity Day, held every March to celebrate the past, present, and future. This themed celebration includes performances, speeches, and presentations; it is attended by current students and alumnae going as far back as the 1960s. After the celebration, some alumnae participate in a luncheon, where there is reconnecting through laughter and taking photos for social media using the hashtag #DoveLove, referring to the school mascot and our admiration for each other. On Unity Day, social media is flooded with pictures!

During my time at Western, I had my own share of drama, which I can chuckle at now. I was popular, with a reputation for being down-to-earth. I got along well with a lot of people and had friends in different circles. And of course, there were besties, too—one of which was my cousin, who lived a block away. On several occasions, we had spats that resulted in us not speaking.

My cousin got her driver's license in the tenth grade and her first car was a gray Nissan Maxima. When she got her car, she drove us back and forth to school. One day, soon after she got the car, I accidently left the back door open. After school, we discovered that the battery was dead. Naturally, we argued about it, and I decided I would go back to driving my mom's car to school. Our mothers got involved and eventually, we got over it.

Again, this was one of a few situations that temporarily interrupted our relationship. This back-and-forth sister-cousin friendship was one where I experienced both the comfort and the heartburn that can come with a female relationship. My entire experience at Western and with my cousin involved lessons of learning about and living sisterhood. I also came to realize the role that personalities play in friendship and connections.

> *Our lives are shaped as profoundly by personality as by gender or race. And the single most important aspect of personality…*
> *is where we fall on the introvert-extrovert spectrum.*
> ~ Susan Cain

Family Are Friends Too

As I reflect on my formative years, I would be remiss not to share about the relationships I had, and continue to have, with the women in my immediate family. There was my mom, grandmothers, two sisters, and a blood cousin who was raised as my niece. Additionally, the relationship I have with my daughter is profound and encourages me to be a model to her for creating and fostering healthy relationships with women. I am close with my cousin who went to Western and she is a major presence in my life. I identify and consider her immediate family. Our relationship has evolved over the years as we grew from teenagers into adult women with children of our own.

 It is in the womb that women form their first relationship. Although we don't remember this, it is powerful because that is when the mother-daughter bond is created. During pregnancy, mothers protect, provide, and prepare for the birth of their baby. The growing fetus depends on the mom's actions, such as eating, taking vitamins, and going to doctors' appointments, to develop. I can't think of any connection that can compare to this. After childbirth and throughout life, the mother-child bond continues to evolve.

I am grateful for the relationship I had with my mother. Although she passed away in 2003, I still love her and cherish the relationship we had. My mom was my best friend, but it was not always that way. When I was growing up, I am certain that she loved me, although at times she did not like me, especially when I was a teenager. I was sassy and thought I knew everything.

While I was at Western, I was head over heels for this guy I was dating, but she was not fond of him. One day, I managed to get out with him, and she did not know where I was. She called his house looking for me and spoke to his mother. His older brother was listening in on a separate phone as his mother explained that she had not seen me and that my boyfriend was not home. Instinctively, my mom put two and two together. That was one of many teenage instances when my mom was undoubtedly sick of me. When I finally got home, I tried to wiggle my way out of it and of course ended up punished. Thank goodness for time, life experience, growth, and maturity.

Our relationship began to blossom into a friendship after I graduated from Western. It was during this time that I began to appreciate the sacrifices my mother and father made for me and my siblings. I started to see what being an adult was like and could relate to her better. She became my advisor, confidante, and cheerleader.

Our friendship grew exponentially when I was pregnant and became a mother and a wife, all in the span of ten months. She helped me learn how to care for my daughter and listened to my numerous marriage issues and everyday life dilemmas. We spent a great deal of time doing family things, such as going to church, celebrating holidays and birthdays, taking bus trips, and eating Sunday dinner. By the way, eating Sunday dinner at my parents' house was just like the Sunday dinner scene in the movie *Soul Food*. My mom and I were not just mom and daughter and best friends; we were soul sisters. This description of our relationship is still not sufficient, as it was soo much more than these words can explain.

My mom suffered from kidney disease and received three-hour dialysis treatments three times a week. When I was in my early thirties, she finally decided to get a kidney transplant. I got tested to be a donor and was happy to do so. That was the least I could do for her to enhance her quality of life, and the decision was easy for me.

I recall her being happy but understandably concerned for me. Naturally, she wondered if I would need dialysis one day because having hereditary high blood pressure contributed to her kidneys failing. After learning that I was a match, she had to go through a series of other tests to prepare for the surgery. Unbeknownst to her, she was put on the donor list and was called to get a kidney twice. Both times, she was in the hospital getting treatment for infections.

Unfortunately, the infections were the beginning of the end of her journey. I wish she would have decided to pursue the transplant sooner. At times, I reflect on what would have become of the kidney transplant surgery. I know that if it were successful, we would have been even closer.

For those of us who are, and have been, fortunate to experience a close and healthy relationship with our mothers, it is a priceless gift and a true blessing. A mother's unconditional love, unending support, wise counsel, and steadfast loyalty enrich a woman's life. It can also give a woman a foundation, a model, and a resource for developing healthy relationships with other women.

Throughout my mother's life, I watched her support female family members and friends by giving them sound advice, providing transportation to work, loaning them money, and caring for their children when no one else was available. Her relationships with women were strong and positive. Everything I experienced through the relationship with my mother and witnessing her own relationships with other women undoubtedly played—and still plays—a significant role in the way I relate to women. Shouting to heaven, "Thank you, Mom!"

As I write about my mother, I hear the sound of her voice. I recall being stopped on the street by strangers asking me my name because of our strong resemblance. They wanted to know if I was her daughter, or they remembered me as a child, had not seen her in a while, and wanted to know how she was doing. My heart beams with pride because I inherited some of her personality traits. She was down-to-earth, made friends everywhere she went, and was loved by many.

For a few years, she worked at the before- and after-school program at the elementary school my siblings and I attended. She loved children and had a special way of connecting with them. When I see people who were a part of the program in person, or post a picture of her on Facebook, they share how she loved them and impacted their lives. Her legacy of being kind, loving, and supportive to people—and women in particular—is inspiring, and makes me proud. Again, shouting to heaven, "Thank you, Mom!"

There are six years between my older sister and me. When we were growing up, she was a cross between a big sister and a second mother. She is a nurturer by nature and by experience. As the eldest child and second mother, she helped my mother with taking care of me and my younger siblings. She learned how to cook, ride the bus, and clean up at an early age. I vividly recall us going to school and she would drop me off and then pick me up and we would go home. She also watched us during the summertime while my parents were at work all day. She answered some of my embarrassing questions about puberty. After she got her driver's license, she became the chauffeur for all of us too.

Some things just don't change about a person. When I became a new mother, my sister supported me by babysitting. In fact, she was one of the few people with whom my daughter would stay without crying. Today, my sister's nurturing spirit still lives; it just looks different. She still cooks for family gatherings and holidays. She still makes herself available in times of need to provide emotional support. When I had the flu a couple years ago, I was completely miserable and home alone. She put the risk of catching the flu aside to help me by spending the night and making sure I had food and something to drink. Most of all, she ensured that I would not suffer alone.

Having a combination big sister-second mother has been a blessing. Over the years, our relationship has had its ups and downs. We have laughed, cried, partied, traveled, and raised our kids together. Sometimes we disagree and have gone weeks without talking. In spite of it all, the journey we have shared as big sister-little sister has enriched my life and contributed to my understanding and practice of sisterhood, compassion, and forgiveness.

There are seven years between my youngest sister and me. She is smart, adventurous, and creative. She has the perfect combination of book smarts and street smarts.

When we were growing up, we were in different worlds. While she was in elementary school and playing with dolls, I was at Western and interested in boys. During that time of my life, my priority was having fun, and the bulk of that was with my peers.

After we were both adults and mothers, our relationship began to grow. We were able to relate to each other and became friends. I am grateful that our relationship blossomed in adulthood. She is also an extrovert and full of life and energy. Her outgoing spirit adds a different dynamic to my life than my oldest sister because we interact like girlfriends.

As sisters and friends, we have also partied, traveled, raised our kids, and celebrated milestones. There have been countless hours spent talking on the phone about our jobs, family, relationships, goals, money, dreams, and disappointments. We have shared happy moments, like attending her graduation from college and the first inauguration of President Barack Obama.

When my sister walked into our parents' house that I renovated, her eyes filled with tears. She expressed that our parents would have been happy with the new look and feel of the house and I beamed with pride. On the other hand, we have also been each other's shoulder to cry on in difficult times. We went through back-to-back divorces. She went through a health scare and had major life-saving surgery. I will always remember that day. I was in the hospital room and the moment before the hospital staff took her to surgery was scary. I cried and hoped for the best. All went well and fortunately, she fully recovered.

My cousin, who was raised as my niece, would best be described as an egg. She is hard on the outside, but once you get to know her, she is a soft sweetheart. Growing up, she had a small circle of friends. She is witty, strong, hardworking, outspoken, and independent. Like my younger sister, when we were growing up, we were in two different worlds. She would be considered the baby of the family. I can recall helping her when we were growing up and babysitting for short periods of time. She followed in my footsteps and went to Western.

I have a funny memory of my cousin that I will never forget. When she was about eight, we were at home alone one day. I was having some trouble using the bathroom and was in pain, screaming to no avail. She came into the bathroom and held my hands. In the middle of my agony, I told her I needed a cigarette and to go get me one. Miraculously, she came back with one. As I sat there smoking, she remained by my side. After a few minutes, I got some relief. I still owe her thanks for enduring that ordeal with me.

Over the years, our relationship has remained as aunt and niece, with a portion of girlfriends. She is a full-grown woman now with a daughter of her own and a granddaughter. She looks to me for support, encouragement, and guidance. I get strength from knowing she leans on me for wisdom, which helps me dig deep to continue to inspire her through my words and deeds.

I did not envision being a mother—not because I did not see myself as mother material; I was just not interested. My dream was to be a career woman and dedicate my energy to that.

However, life and love have a way of changing things, and even today, I am still in awe of how I embraced motherhood. I recall comments from my mother and maternal grandmother, who both were utterly shocked about the mother I became. (I guess I wasn't the only one who did not think motherhood would be a part of my life.)

While I was pregnant, I was fascinated by the developing person in my womb. I was in college at that time and would go to the campus library to read a book that described the development of a fetus. The book also had vivid images. As I read the stages of fetal growth and viewed the pictures, I imagined how my baby was growing inside of me. I wanted a boy and thought for sure that was what I would deliver. I wanted a boy because I figured we would be close and he would one day take care of me. I had only one sonogram and the baby's legs were crossed, so I had no way of knowing I was having a girl.

My experience as a mother has been filled with joy, fear, love, pride, gratitude, and some stress. I credit my daughter's birth with adding to my sense of urgency to grow up. When she was born, I was the tender age of twenty-one and still developing as a young adult. Knowing and accepting that I would be responsible for her life forced me to mature. My goal was to be the best mother I could be, with the hope of raising a God-fearing, moral, loving, responsible, well-rounded, and productive woman. I believed and hoped that how I raised her— along with how I conducted myself—would shape her life. I was intentional about introducing her to Christianity, devoting a lot of quality time with her and exposing her to culture. We spent a lot of time with my family, and she was involved in modeling, dancing, and acting. There were also family trips and plenty of celebrations.

My hopes became reality. My daughter is adventurous, headstrong, outspoken, creative, and brave. She reminds me of a boss. She has studied and still lives abroad. We are both friendly and have a spirit of determination. I admire her strength and courage. She is living her life out loud and unapologetically. We get along well and support each other.

At this phase in our mother-daughter journey, our relationship is mixed. I am still a loving and overprotective mother that freely and often provides wisdom and guidance, while simultaneously giving her space to make decisions for her life. There is a growing element of friendship between us. I am happy and fulfilled with where we are today.

We called our maternal grandmother Gran. She passed away when I was in my early twenties, and I think of her almost every day. She was an independent, strong, hardworking, no-nonsense type of woman. She was all that and a good provider. When she was growing up in the 1930s and 1940s, it was expected for a woman to be a mother and wife. Not Gran. She was an unwed single mother and trained as a nurse. She was determined to provide a comfortable life for herself and my mom. She owned a home in Northwest Baltimore. She made a living as a private duty nurse and was also an LPN at Crownsville Hospital Center, a (now closed) psychiatric hospital.

When I was growing up, Gran helped my parents by watching us, and at one time, we even lived with her. She demanded respect and managed us with some fear. Along with the fear, there was love.

When I reflect on our interactions during the early years of my life, I remember being disciplined, and I also remember her picking me up from school and taking me to work with her. At the time, she was taking care of an elderly lady in her home. I enjoyed this time with Gran because we would talk and have fun. There was a chairlift on the stairs at her patient's house and Gran used to ride me up and down like it was a carnival ride.

When Gran found out I was pregnant, she called me to have a heart-to-heart conversation. I honored and revered her. I did not want to disappoint her and was gravely concerned about what she would say and think. To my surprise, she gave me some advice I will never forget. She said, "Live your dreams." She must have known that I needed to hear those words to support my motivation to not only make a life for myself, but to live my best life. I believe that conversation was a turning point in our relationship.

After my daughter was born, Gran and I became more friendly, and I relied on her experience as a nurse to help me with taking care of my baby girl when she was ill. One time, my daughter had a fever, I called Gran and she told me to wipe her down with alcohol to break the fever. What a home remedy that was! And just one of many. During that time in my life, I was struggling financially and would call on her to get me out of back-against-the-wall binds. She always came through with loans or just giving me money for groceries, Pampers, gas, rent, and utilities.

When she passed away suddenly, I had my first bout of anxiety, and it was crippling. I was traumatized. For months, I did not want to do anything alone because I feared I would die at any moment. Being around others constantly offered comfort. I felt if I were about to die, the person or people in my presence could stop it.

Over time, I got better, and the anxiety subsided. The anxiety and the grief added to my realization of just how much Gran meant to me and how special our relationship had become. Today, I remain grateful for her support, guidance, wisdom, and example of being an independent woman.

My paternal grandmother had a quiet spirit, and she was somewhat bashful. She got a divorce when her children were young and raised them on her own. My dad was her second-born, and there was a gap between him and his six younger siblings. My youngest aunt is only nine years older than me.

When I was growing up, I spent time with my grandmother, and my aunts and uncles were there too. We did a lot of family things together, like going to church, visiting the beach, and celebrating holidays, so I did not have time with her alone, but I know she loved me. When I got pregnant, she was concerned, and checked on me often. One day, she brought me a bagful of fruit because she wanted to make sure I was eating properly.

When I was a young adult, I moved into a neighborhood close to where my grandmother lived. In fact, my youngest aunt lived across the street. At that time, our relationship grew, and we interacted one-on-one. The bulk of our conversations were over the phone. I used to call her, and we would talk about what was going on with family members, and I would tease her about her dating life. She actually dated an elderly gentleman who lived across the street from me. I was amazed at her zest and energy.

She got a kick out of the questions I asked her, and we enjoyed plenty of laughs. If I needed her for anything she was always there and was particularly supportive with my daughter. When my daughter was in high school, she would experience unbearable pain at a certain time of the month. Since my grandmother lived close by, she would pick her up from school while I was at work.

There are some forms of support that are invaluable, and the way she supported me is one of them. She has gone on to glory as well, but she left me with precious memories of joyful conversations and an example of being committed to faith.

My mother's nickname for my cousin was The Girl From Africa, from the movie *Coming to America*, which, coincidentally, is one of my favorite comedy movies of all time. There is one scene when Eddie Murphy's character, Prince Hakeem, and Arsenio Hall's character, Semmi, approach the door outside the barbershop and Eddie Murphy's other character, Clarence, says, "Hey! It's the boys from Africa." The connection between my cousin and the movie is fitting because she has a great sense of humor.

Aside from being humorous, my cousin is a straight shooter, smart, hardworking, stylish, fun, loving, kind, and strong. We have been up, down, and all around together. Just like my sisters, we have raised our children together, partied, traveled, attended family functions, and shopped, but the number one thing we do is talk. In fact, we speak on the phone almost every morning and never run out of things to discuss.

Her sons have learned a lot about family history, women, relationships, working, and life in general from our daily conversations, which were mostly when she was driving to work. We support each other. We encourage each other. We celebrate each other. We love each other. I am deeply grateful for her—sometimes in unexpected ways.

Recently, I had a snake in my basement. It was close to midnight, and I ran out of my house in my pajamas, carrying only my car keys and cell phone. I called her, terrified, and planned to sleep in my car. She told me to come to her house to spend the night, even though this was during the COVID-19 pandemic. I went, and she made sure I was comfortable. This is just one of the many ways she has been there for me. I remain grateful.

I described the personalities and dynamics of the relationships I have had and continue to have with the women in my family because my experiences with them helped to shape me, which in turn impacts how I relate to and treat other women. I have learned to accept a woman as she is and for who she is. Not only that, but I hold myself accountable for my own actions and practice forgiveness. Self-reflecting, holding my feet to the fire, processing disappointments, and getting over them with my family has added to my sisterhood journey with other women and how I treat my friends.

The best part of life is when your family become your friends and your friends become your family.
~ Robin Roberts

Sisterhood and the Words We Speak

When women get together, they talk about work, family, popular culture, politics, dating, goals, dreams, fears, church—you name it. These conversations can leave them laughing, thinking, empowered, relieved, encouraged, strengthened, crying, and everything in between. Talking is one way that women form bonds, and it is a beautiful thing. As a natural talker, I can attest to the power of conversation, especially when it is authentic, heartfelt, uplifting, informative, and even humorous. What is the first thing women do when they get good news? They call a family member or friend to share it. Or they wait until a gathering to share the news in person. Those experiences are cherished.

On the other hand, there are conversations that entail women talking *about* each other in a negative manner. I am not referring to the conversations that offer a safe place to vent about a situation that caused frustration, disappointment, or confusion. Or when a woman is speaking matter-of-factly. We can easily discern when words are spoken out of concern, hurt, or empathy versus out of hostility, spite, and resentment. Those shoulder-to-lean-on discussions are understandable and healthy. It is another story when the conversation is malicious on any level. Women sometimes have a habit of gossiping, judging, tearing each other down, and dragging each other's names through the mud. Often, it is done without awareness because it is so commonplace. It is not just the words that are said, but the body language and tone that accompany them. Sometimes, those mean conversations are sought out and can become the foundation, focus, or glue for some people's relationships. Unfortunately, talking about one another negatively is embedded in society, to the point of being enjoyed, entertaining, and monetized. To make it even worse, there are times when we smile in someone's face while pretending or suppressing that we spoke negatively about them. All of that is deeply concerning. I believe when words are spoken in a poisonous way, it reveals something deeper about the person who utters them. Perhaps they are angry, bitter, jealous, insecure, unhappy, bored, opinionated, messy, or plotting to take someone down or ruin their reputation.

I am expressing this not to point fingers. I have been engaged in conversations in which I have heard women say ugly things about another woman they identified as a friend. On a few occasions, I spoke up and expressed my opinion that the dialogue was wrong. In other situations, I froze because I was in shock, caught off guard, or hurt by what I heard. I am non-confrontational and take time to process what I hear. I acknowledge that speaking out in these situations is something I have struggled with and need to work on.

Take a moment to envision yourself as a ghost in a room full of women you know and love, and they are speaking badly about you or judging your actions and decisions. Consider how that would make you feel and then, going forward, allow that realization to be your guide when it comes to choosing your words about others.

Words are powerful and can take on a life of their own. What is spoken aloud represents what is in the heart and on the mind. Before speaking negatively about other women, take time to reflect and soul search. Words can be weapons when used to say bad things about other women or put them down. Make a commitment to yourself to be mindful of your words and refrain from saying anything negative. Focus on words that heal, uplift, inspire, and encourage to sow seeds into sisterhood.

Resist talking about people. Gossip is one of the worst practices.
~ Harriette Cole

Men Can Impact Sisterhood

One of my dearest friends has been in my life for more than twenty years. We are close, and although we are not blood relatives, I regard her as family. She knows my entire family and has spent a considerable amount of time with them.

After I separated from my ex-husband, my friend and I were catching up over the phone. We were talking about the separation, and she dropped a bombshell, sharing that she saw him out in public with a woman while we were together. I presumed it was his mistress. She explained that she approached them and inquired about me and my daughter's whereabouts. Naturally, my first question was, "Why didn't you tell me?" She relayed that she did not want to contribute to or be responsible for the marriage ending.

I felt disappointed, angry, and embarrassed. I felt disappointed, because I thought she would have told me something like that. I felt embarrassed about her knowing this for a period of time, interacting with me, and me not knowing what she had seen. I also thought about how men who are openly unfaithful put others—especially their wife's friends they run into in public—in awkward and difficult situations.

I explained to my friend that I wished she would have told me, and I would not have been angry with her. Since I understood her concern about impacting the marriage, this did not interfere with or negatively impact our relationship. I let it go.

This scenario is common. Oftentimes, when a friend shares such information, the relationship can and does get ugly. One way to avoid a problem is to have a conversation with friends about what they would want you to do if you saw their mate with someone else. That way, if it happens, everyone will know what to expect.

Of course, when it comes to situations with the opposite sex that can impact female relationships, it doesn't matter how old you are. As human beings, we are wired from a young age to desire romantic relationships and the love that can come along with them. Love is a powerful force that most of us have difficulty quantifying and describing adequately. It makes us feel good emotionally and can be intoxicating.

Because of love's matchless force, I understand why women and girls often find themselves in unhealthy situations, including having arguments and even physical fights over men and boys. When I was around thirteen years old, I was involved in a physical fight that centered around a boy—although I took the position that I was not fighting over him, but to defend myself against another girl who approached me first.

The boy lived in Hilltop and had a girlfriend. In fact, she was a friend of mine and also lived in Hilltop. We hung out and socialized together in the same neighborhood group. They both lived on the same block, and my block was parallel to theirs. He and I used to play basketball in the alley we shared, and it started out innocently enough. Then, after a few nights of playing basketball, we started flirting. The flirting led to some kissing.

I don't know how she learned that we were playing basketball and had kissed. There was some he-said-she-said, and it got back to me that she wanted to fight. I was expecting it to happen, and two of my besties vowed that if we fought and any of her besties got into the fight, they would as well.

The day came when she'd obviously had enough and knocked on my door, inviting me to take a walk to the store. I had my two besties with me, and she had one. Before we made it to the end of my block, we were arguing. We continued heading through the alley and ended up beside a neighborhood bar. By this time, of course, the argument had escalated.

I remember the ground was covered with broken glass and pebbles. What I can't remember is who threw the first punch. We were hitting each other in the face and then slipped and fell to the ground. I recall using as much of my strength as I could to punch her in the face as we rolled around the rocky ground. She ended up on top of me and bit my eyelid. I screamed and pushed her off me. That's when the fight ended. My eye was swollen and I had scratches on my body from the rough ground.

As I returned home with my besties, they told me I had won the fight, but another observer proclaimed it was a tie. The sad truth, unbeknownst to us at the time, was that we both lost. First, a crime was committed. Second, our behavior sent a message that it was okay to fight because of a boy. Third, we lost our sisterhood.

Fortunately, my eyelid healed and she was okay. However, although we were young and immature, we never should have fought, and I hold my teenage self accountable for flirting and kissing my friend's boyfriend. I am not proud of this, but also realize that, as a teenager, I lacked wisdom.

Sadly, women and girls sometimes get into physical fights that leave them injured or even killed. This is deeply disturbing and sad. Sometimes these fights are recorded and glorified on social media. That is why it is critical for teen girls to learn about valuing themselves and each other. It is also important for them to learn about the value of sisterhood as early as possible. I am grateful that my childhood friend and I moved on and put the entire situation behind us. Today, we are Facebook friends and I recently spoke to her about what happened. We went down memory lane and caught up about our lives. It was a great conversation, and we promised to get together soon.

Whatever the scenario, the lessons remain the same for girls and women everywhere: tangled, tumultuous relationships with boys and men are unhealthy and damaging, both to them and their connections with others. And however enticing romantic relationships may be, in the end, sisterhood should be a priority, and is a powerful force to be reckoned with.

Because there's one thing stronger than magic: sisterhood.
~ Robin Benway

Sisterhood on the Job

When I was sixteen, I got my very first job at Burger King and my salary was $2.85 an hour. A friend from Western worked there, told me they were hiring, and gave me a good reference. I got my second job at McDonald's the same exact way, with help from a friend. Later, while I was in college, I began my career with the federal government.

In my first position, I had an awesome and supportive supervisor. She was applying for an internal position and asked me and my colleagues if one of us could help her with the application. I happily said yes and assisted with the development of it. Unfortunately, she did not get the position she applied for, but she did land another one that she was happy with.

Helping her with that application was the beginning of my own efforts to support women in the workplace with their career advancement. I have assisted other women by sharing job announcements, editing resumes, and conducting mock interviews. I have always wanted to see women succeed. I have also been supported and encouraged by numerous women throughout my entire career.

I believe women need each other to get through life—and that includes their lives on the job as well, because an enormous amount of time is spent working. Aside from their work hours, many women have spent a great deal of time and money preparing for their careers by going to college and pursuing other energy-consuming career initiatives. We all go to work to earn a living, fulfill career aspirations, and provide for ourselves and our families. The workplace is one of the last places on earth a woman should have issues, especially at the hands of another woman.

At one point, I found myself in a work situation that felt like a living hell. I had a female supervisor who gave me and some other female colleagues a hard time, and there were numerous instances when she did things that were not fair or right. She once accused me of not forwarding an email to a colleague, although she did not ask me about it or have any proof. Her tone in the email she sent me was nasty and rude. After receiving her email, I shared the email I sent to the colleague with her. I never received an apology.

Her actions were not egregious enough to warrant legal action, but since I was always a dedicated employee, easygoing, and completed tasks well, I could not understand why she treated me and the other women in such an offensive manner. I consistently received good performance appraisals and was never written up or received any verbal warnings. Other colleagues who witnessed her behavior were equally perplexed. I realize that in all situations involving more than one person, there are two sides to the story, but I would bet my life that her side would not be true or justifiable.

This situation caused me a great deal of stress for several years. I applied for other positions to get relief and did get interviewed but was not selected. I was stuck because there was an internal hiring freeze, and I could not afford to quit. During these difficult times, there were other women who listened, prayed, and provided me with sound advice. Their support helped me get through the challenge, and this painful experience provided powerful and valuable lessons.

I learned that if I were ever in a leadership position, I would treat other women with dignity, respect, and compassion, but I would do that anyway, regardless of my role. I also learned that a key component to leadership is understanding the strengths, weaknesses, and communication styles of people that are being led. Each person is different and processes information in their own way.

It is imperative for female leaders to treat their staff members equally, but individually. It is not wise to make a woman feel as if her livelihood is in jeopardy. Life is already hard enough, and women have faced equal pay issues and other career challenges, especially working mothers. Work-related stress can have a direct impact on one's physical and mental well-being, negatively affecting the way a woman interacts with her family and friends. Furthermore, it can lead to low morale, gossip, and decreased productivity in the workplace.

Sisterhood calls for women, especially women in leadership positions, to lead without being unfair, insensitive, or competitive in an unhealthy way. The goal should be to support and inspire one another to reach goals and work in harmony. I am wise enough to realize that miscommunication, poor performance, and rule-breaking occurs, but I assert and believe that all of that can be addressed without mistreatment or being mean to one's colleagues or employees.

Whether they are just starting off in their first job or working their way up the corporate ladder, if all women were to the extend helping hands of sisterhood to one another, we would all succeed.

Real fearless and fierce women compliment other women,
and we recognize and embrace that their shine in
no way diminishes our light and that it actually
makes our light shine brighter.
~ Gabrielle Union

Sisterhood on the Road

Just as I was finishing up writing this, I had another amazing experience with sisterhood that proved its reach all around the world. I visited Italy during the summer of 2021. Initially, I was planning to visit my daughter in Budapest, Hungary, but my plans changed because my friend who was traveling with me could not get into Budapest because of their COVID-19 travel restrictions. My friend and I were sitting at the gate at Newark International Airport, drinking a fruity beverage from Starbucks and waiting to board the plane to Milan. We were not supposed to be there because our flight from Dulles International Airport the day before had been canceled.

While we were waiting, a woman nearby inquired where the Starbucks was located and I shared the directions. When she commented that she did not want to miss the flight, I asked her for her name and told her I would hold the plane for her. She took off and returned with a beverage from somewhere else because she couldn't find Starbucks and wanted to hurry.

After boarding the plane, I did not see her again until we landed. We started talking as we walked through the airport in Milan. She explained that she was going to the center of the city by train. My friend and I were planning to catch a cab, which would have cost more than the train fare. She offered to help us get our train ticket and show us the way. We gratefully accepted, and on our way to Milan, she explained that she was going to Venice the next day. So were we!

After about an hour-long train ride, we all arrived at the center of Milan. When we disembarked, we started taking selfies and appeared to be lifelong friends. She proceeded to help us get roundtrip train tickets to Venice for the same time she would be traveling, then put our hotel in her cell phone to help us find it. As it turned out, her hotel was across the street from ours. We exchanged phone numbers and made plans to meet up for breakfast the next day.

Early the next morning, she generously bought breakfast for me and my friend at the train station, which was deeply appreciated. She had a full itinerary planned and when we asked if we could tag along, she happily said yes. When we boarded the train, we took more selfies, discussed what we were going to do in Venice, and talked about our lives.

The three of us had a glorious time touring Venice all day long. We laughed, shopped, took plenty of pictures, ate lunch, and enjoyed a gondola ride.

After we got back to Milan, we decided to get dressed up and go to dinner, where we continued our good conversation, laughter, picture taking, and sharing food and more information about our lives. Afterward, we strolled the area and enjoyed getting to know one another and Milan. She was leaving to go back the next morning, so we said our goodbyes at the end of the night and promised to keep in touch.

At some point while we were together, I mentioned the Facebook group, Girls LOVE Travel®, where women share travel information and pictures. I sent her an invite to join the group and she wrote a heartwarming story of how we met and shared photos of our trip. That made my heart smile. As I write this, we have been in touch and she will be visiting us in Baltimore in a few months.

I was having a conversation with my editor about my vacation, and when she asked me if anything happened on my trip that should be in this story, I wanted to scream out loud in excitement! I shared the story about meeting my new sister friend and relayed that she was kind, fun, and contributed to the magic of our trip. This is an example of the power, beauty, and blessing of sisterhood. She did not have to help us navigate to Milan, buy us breakfast, or spend time with us in Venice. We started out as total strangers and ended our time together with precious memories and the promise of sisterhood.

I would be remiss if I did not mention that my friend and I met another woman and her husband in the Dulles International Airport who were booked on the same flight that was canceled. While we were waiting to find out the status of the flight, we talked about our lives and traveling. They were going home to Germany, but once lived in Italy, and gave us good advice about what to see and do there. We had a great conversation and lots of laughs for about two hours. The wife and I exchanged phone numbers and connected on Facebook. Throughout our trip to Italy and their trip back to Germany, we were checking in on each other. She is also one of my new sister friends and we have been keeping in touch.

One last point about my trip to Italy. The friend I went with was the same friend I mentioned earlier who did not go on another trip with me. Things always have a way of working out. We planned this trip mainly to visit my daughter. The three of us bonded and created memories that will last forever.

I am happy to know that the universal magic of sisterhood can be found and nourished anywhere that two or more women of any age happen to be, connecting us all around the globe and uniting us even as we travel to unfamiliar places.

Sometimes when we meet people we feel a connection,
a sense of sisterhood. And usually that sense is correct.
~ Catherine Pulsifer

Sisterhood Is Valuable

I wrote this portion of the book to share pieces of my dance with sisterhood. I use the word *dance* to describe it because, just like life, my experience has had ebbs and flows and continues to unfold. My personality, years growing up in Hilltop, experiences at Western, and relationships with family and friends all provide insight on how sisterhood has choreographed my life.

The overwhelming support and love I have received can't be adequately expressed or quantified. I have shared my story in hopes that hearts, minds, and actions will change regarding sisterhood. Female friendships are important, and how women treat each other matters. I deeply value sisterhood and female friendships. Again, I can't get through life without them.

My friends and family have been there to help me navigate growing in faith, getting an education, raising my daughter, advancing in my career, surviving a divorce, dating, losing loved ones, and traveling through everyday life dilemmas and joys. I am fortunate and have been immensely blessed by numerous amazing women in big and small ways. I wish I could, but I can't even count or name them all in this book. I am deeply grateful for all the ways they poured themselves into my heart and continue to add to my life.

I dream of being able to treat a large group of my sister friends to an all-expenses-paid vacation so we can bond, enjoy spa treatments, eat good food, sightsee, and party. It is also an honor—and I don't take it lightly—to be a friend to many and contribute love, support, compassion, and joy to them. I believe women who have not experienced the joys and blessings of sisterhood, or who have had bad experiences, should take a chance and open themselves up. For those who have been blessed with friends who love, support, and celebrate them, I encourage continued and consistent cultivation of those relationships, as they will enrich life forever. My sentiments are backed up by studies indicating that we are happier and live more fulfilling lives because of our relationships.

You understand that at the end of the day, everything that matters comes down to people and relationships: the people you love and the people who love you.
~ Sophia Nelson

Tips for Living an "I Am My Sister's Keeper" Lifestyle

1. Pray for your friends' health, family, career, finances, goals, and dreams.

2. Do not compete. Everything that is meant for you to achieve and acquire in life will come to fruition.

3. Keep your word and promises. Be intentional about doing what you say you will do. If there is a change in plans or a delay, communicate so expectations will be clear and known.

4. Be supportive. There are numerous ways to be supportive, including listening, being present, reaching out, lending a helping hand, offering advice, and sharing information.

5. Do not be judgmental. Refrain from condemning and being critical. Show compassion, be empathetic, and try to understand the reason or the why behind what is being judged.

6. Celebrate success. Genuinely acknowledge and be happy when a personal or professional goal has been reached.

7. Forgive. If there has been an offense, process it, learn from it, communicate it lovingly, and let it go.

8. Be yourself. Know yourself and love yourself so you can show up exactly as you are.

9. Watch your words. Think before you speak. Do not say things that are rude, presumptuous, hurtful, mean, or inaccurate about other women or to them.

10. Respect. Show regard for others' family, feelings, beliefs, thoughts, and property.

11. Do not say or do things to put yourself on a pedestal, to make yourself appear better, or put another woman down.

12. Do not plot and/or take actions to destroy a woman's family, finances, career, or reputation.

13. Keep in touch. Periodically and consistently send text messages, emails, or handwritten notes to say hello, check in, share updates, and express love.

14. Be serious and intentional about spending quality time together and creating memories. Plan brunch, lunch, dinner, exercise,

spa treatments, shopping, girls' trips, attending church, or whatever activity you enjoy.

15. Love. Treat those close to you as well as strangers the way you want to be treated. Take the high road. Remember that sisterhood is a verb, and be your sister's keeper!

Movement Step, Action Step

Follow the tips above to create and cultivate healthy relationships. Learn what your love language is to determine the ways you show and receive love. Knowing your love language will help guide your relationships with women. Visit www.5lovelanguages.com.

Success is Never by Accident

Deidra Bass

I can do all things through Christ who strengthens me.
~ Philippians 4:13, NKJV

Success is never by accident. It's a series of small decisions and steps made over time. It starts with making an initial decision to go for it, followed by intentionality, consistency, and commitment. This is the true recipe that I've found for success. You have to first make the decision to succeed and then become absolutely intentional about it.

Once you make a decision to succeed, you have to go after it with everything you've got, blocking out any and all distractions as much as possible. Again, you must be intentional about it.

I believe you must define a thing before you can do a thing. So know that *intentional* is an action word, meaning to be purposeful, done *on* purpose and with purpose! It's synonymous with words like *deliberate* and *willful*. Those are not passive words, those are active words, meaning requiring action on your part. You have to do something. I love the term *being done with purpose* because it's not haphazard, it's not by chance, but done with intention and an end goal in mind.

Next, after making a decision and being purposeful, you have to be consistent. Know up front that consistency and convenience are typically at odds with one another. *Consistent* means following the same principles and course of action repeatedly. It's synonymous with words like *steady, reliable, constant,* and *unwavering.* That just sounds dependable and reliable, and exactly what we need in business and in life. Who would not want to do business with a dependable business or person?

This is especially true in the world of constant change and flux. Believe it or not, this was one area I struggled with the most. I would start a project, work on it a few hours or weeks, and then stop and not work on it again for days or sometimes weeks at a time! I was very inconsistent, which decreased my productivity and my results. The exact opposite of what I was going for. I found when I was inconsistent, I actually lost time! Go figure.

Time is a very precious and valuable commodity, and once it's lost, you can't get it back. During past times of inconsistency, I had to re-acclimate and re-learn because you either use it or you lose it, which caused even more lost time. Again, the exact opposite of the results I wanted.

What helped me was realizing I didn't need large chunks of time, I just needed to be consistent with the chunks of time I worked. At first, I was trying to block off unrealistic hours at a time, I knew I could not fulfill the commitment due to other responsibilities. I made a mental adjustment and blocked off realistic pockets of time, like an hour or two, or my lunch break, and became consistent with that. Times that I identified as "grind and go get it" focused time where I had to work, whether I felt like it or not.

I had to say no to binge-watching TV shows, being on the phone, or any activity that did not align with what I needed to accomplish at that time. I literally found fifteen hours in my week just by turning the television off to work my business. You can't be tossed about with every wind or distraction; that's considered unstable and undependable, not to mention you will get very little done.

You have to be consistent in season and out of season, whether you feel like it or not. Success is never based on feelings. You have to have a purpose bigger than your feelings because sometimes you just won't feel like it. There were plenty of times I did not feel like working my business. I remember times my girlfriends were planning get-togethers, and I was working on hitting particular goals and had to decline on multiple occasions. But I knew my hard work and diligence up front would pay off later, and it absolutely did! I hit my goals and grew my business. I knew there would be plenty of time to play later and have something to celebrate. I'm a firm believer in working hard and playing hard. Consistency reminds me of the phrase, "Steady as she goes," holding the course, as one of my mentors would say.

Consistency, for instance, in the sales world would be making 10 new contacts a day or seventy contacts a week, or reading one book a month, or in ministry, inviting five new guests a week. The key is to do what you do consistently; if you say you are going to do something, you do it. If you are going to dedicate an hour or two to a task on Tuesdays and Thursdays, then commit to it and do it. Block that time out on your calendar.

My family knew when I went into the home office and closed the door that it was "Do Not Disturb" work time. On certain days and at certain times, they knew not to plan anything for me; that was business time and they respected it. They knew Wednesday nights was Bible study time. That's how you have to be with your business. If you put everything before your business, your business will become the sacrifice.

You have to be intentional and make time for the things that matter. It does not have to be a lot of time, to where it's overwhelming and you neglect something else, but you do have to prioritize and set aside time for worthwhile things consistently and intentionally. Being consistent adds a structure and dependability that produces results. You can't be haphazard with your goals and dreams.

If you really want to increase your results, add an accountability partner to help keep you accountable and not accept excuses. Again, it can't be dependent on feelings; feelings can change like the weather. Your business, your goals, your passion will suffer or, at best, have mediocre or diminished results. However, if you are consistent, they will thrive. *You* will thrive! You will reach your goals. You can accomplish more with a consistent one to two hours, three times a week, than an inconsistent block of time every now and then.

Let's not forget commitment. Commitment is key. Life is going to happen! Trust me. As I've heard said, "Just keep on living." The changes of life will not stop. Things are going to come up, pop up, and rear up (and most likely during the most inopportune times) that you did not expect or were looking for, but you have to find a way and the will to push through anyhow. This is where the saying "Where there's a will, there's a way" rings truer than ever. I mean, who expected a global pandemic called COVID-19 to put the entire world on pause? Not me. Neither did anyone else.

Commitment will keep you rooted and grounded and tied to your goals, decisions, and ultimately, to your success, even when life is happening all around you. Control the things you can control. You may have to pivot or make some adjustments, but your commitment will keep you going.

Not too long after I started my business, my husband became sick. I had to curtail in-person business trips and travel so I could be home, and I had to work virtually and leverage the people around me to assist. But I did not stop. I did not quit. I just had to be more creative with how and when I worked. If you say you are going to do something for a year or 18 months, give it that time and stay committed to that decision for that duration, through the ups and downs, highs and lows, successes and failures. The key is to remain committed, pivot, and adjust accordingly.

It's critical to have a time period tied to your commitment. Give yourself time to succeed. Too many people give up so easily and quickly. I'm always wary of get-rich-quick schemes because I know there is nothing quick about success, and it's definitely not easy. Anything successful requires time and effort. Without a time commitment, you may shortchange yourself and throw in the towel too soon, right before you reach your goal.

I had a mentor tell me once that goals without dates are just hopes, and hope is not a good success strategy in and of itself. Remember, success is not just about the destination, but the journey along the way. It requires commitment and time for recovery, resilience, learning, and growth. Time to learn, time to grow, time to make mistakes, time to learn from those mistakes, time to reflect, time to make adjustments, time to give your dreams and goals a chance to succeed.

Often, we just give up too soon, when success is right around the corner—one step away, one connection away, one call or text away, and one prayer away. Don't give up. Our dreams are worth it, and so are you. Plus, who you develop into and who you find along the way—yourself—is absolutely worth it!

Remember to also celebrate small successes and victories along the way. When I made my first $300 in business, you would have thought it was $3 million! My first year in business, I only made approximately $5,000. Again, you would have thought I hit the lottery. I celebrated those small profits because I knew the process worked and I had not quit. So don't wait for the grand finale or the ultimate success, although it will be something to shout about and worthy of celebration. It could take a while, so to combat weariness or the temptation to give up and throw in the towel, celebrate small milestones and successes on the way to the Big One. Celebrate small wins and achievements that are all building blocks to your success. Remember those things that you said no to earlier while you were blocking distractions? Now you can say yes to them and celebrate.

Remember: make a decision, be intentional, be consistent, and be committed. Success will follow, not by accident, but on purpose, through intentionality, consistency, and commitment. Go for it. Success awaits, and you and your dreams and your family are worth it.

VIP Access Only

We've all heard of a VIP (Very Important Person), right? It invokes feelings of special privileges and special access, like front-row seats, backstage passes, special arrangements, or special seating. It usually entails some type of extra cost or "who you know." VIP is special. It's not for everyone. Everyone does not have VIP access. If they did, the term *VIP* would lose its value. When something becomes common or not special, it starts to lose its value.

When it comes to your dreams, you have to allow only VIP access. You have to avoid the dream killers. You have to allow limited access, VIP access only, to your dreams and goals.

I had to learn this the hard way, and it caused me some deep hurt but a much-needed lesson. Not everyone I shared my dreams of entrepreneurship with were excited or happy or rooting for me. Some well-meaning people, even some of the closest people to me—and I have to admit, it hurt and stung initially. I expected full support from those I knew and loved and who loved me, but some did not understand my drive or my dreams of entrepreneurship and financial and time freedom. I had to become OK with that because my vision was not their vision, nor were my dreams their dreams.

Some people could be very well-meaning and loving people, and just not understand. That does not make them bad, it just makes them people with differing goals, priorities, and dreams, and again, that's okay. Some people could be family members, friends, church members, coworkers, or just haters, you name it. Some people may not support you because it does not align with their agendas or plans for you, or it takes time away from them, or they just don't get it and I say again, that is okay. What you cannot do is let that deter you and your pursuit of your dreams and goals because at the end of the day, it's *your* dream, it's *your* vision, not theirs. We have to be okay with not everyone supporting us or understanding our drive or ambition, because it's not their dream or vision, it's yours. They may not understand the purpose that's inside you, so you have to protect your dreams and God-given purpose at all costs, especially from the dream killers.

Dream killers can come in many forms, to include naysayers, negativity, and non-support. You have to allow limited access and protect your dream like a precious baby, because your dream *is* precious. Think about how you would protect your child; you wouldn't allow just anyone around him or her. You wouldn't take him/her to certain environments. You would make sure they were in healthy, productive, and protected environments.

You have to protect your dream or vision the same way. You can't share it with everyone. You can't take it around everyone, and you can't take it to toxic, unhealthy, or non-supportive environments. You need to be in supportive environments where it can thrive and grow—limited VIP access only, especially in the early incubation stages.

Dream killers in the form of naysayers may say you can't do it. They may say that for a number of reasons, like fear or their own insecurity. What they mean is *they* can't do it—and they are probably right! They can't or they won't, so they try to project their feelings onto you. But you can't let that stop, deter, or kill your dream. The dream was not given to them, so they may be perfectly right; they can't do it. Guess what? You can! My Bible tells me, in Philippians 4:13, "I can do All things through Christ." I'm going with what God says any day over what people say.

When I first started my business, some of those closest to me did not support it. They viewed anything other than what they wanted me to do or my complete availability to them as sinful, or somehow not being as committed. It really hurt! But I developed some thick skin and learned to divorce myself from the opinions of others because they are just that, opinions, and that's none of your business. Other people's opinions are none of your business.

Dream killers in the form of negative people show up differently. They may just never have anything positive to say. Have you ever met someone who just sucks the life out of the room when they show up? I mean, negative just to be negative? Of course, we all have. You have to be careful not to let them suck the life out of your dream—and you. You say it's a beautiful, sunny day, they say it's too hot. You say it's a beautiful winter wonderland, they say it's too cold. You say take time to smell the roses, and they say they are allergic. There's just no positive vibes coming from them.

I'm a firm believer that your vibe attracts your tribe, and your tribe attracts your vibe. I also believe "the Power of Life and Death is in the tongue." That's a verse out of the Bible (Proverbs 18:21); it simply means positive words bring life and negative words bring death to ideas, to confidence, to dreams, to belief, if you allow them to. So protect your dream at all costs. Don't let someone else's negativity plant seeds of doubt in your mind. You'll have to limit their access to you, "only VIP access."

As you grow, you may find yourself granting less and less access until it becomes no access. That's a decision you'll have to make based on other aspects of the relationship. If they are negative just in this area, then you will have to set clear boundaries, because this is important to you. And you'll need to let them know at least if they don't have anything positive to say, not to say anything negative, and because this is important to you, then they need to respect it. Period.

Non-supportive people are dream killers who may just not be there for you, at least not in the way you expect them to be or in the way you've been there for them. They are noticeably absent. This can be very hurtful. It definitely was to me. I was someone who always tried to support my friends as much as I could. If it meant I had back-to-back commitments or triple commitments in a given day, or if something was important to a close friend, I would be there.

I recall times when I got off the airplane, just returning to town, to support graduation parties, birthday parties, anniversary parties, a revival, outreach, etc., before I even went home. If it was special to them, then it was special to me, and if I gave my word to be there to support them, then I would be there.

I remember a particular time getting off a plane and instead of coming home, where I wanted to be because I was exhausted, I went to my friend's anniversary luncheon. It hurt when this was not reciprocated in some of my relationships, when I started my business and some of those close to me did not show up or support me with just their presence; again, it hurt.

However, I got the greatest gift to myself. It freed me up to start saying no and to stop overcommitting myself to them. If they could say no, then I could too, and I did, which freed up more of my time. Now I had those ride-or-die friends who were there to support me, even if in presence only.

Another thing you want to pay attention to are those who don't clap for you when you win; that's more telling than you know. All you can ask of these people is that if they can't support you, then at least they do not try to hinder you. Get them out of the way and do your thing. You've got this, and you don't need permission to do it.

Avoid the dream killers at all costs! Your dreams need you to show up in full force, not on life support and debilitated because you gave VIP access to the wrong people, who sucked the life out of them and you. Remember, your dream is all yours, so nourish it and protect it as such. Feed it good things, not negativity; take it to good, supportive, and protected environments, around other like-minded, goal-oriented people with proven success and watch it grow and thrive. I once heard the great Bishop TD Jakes say, "Everyone does not get a seat in your front row." I couldn't agree more!

Your Front Row

Front-row seating is primo seating, similar to VIP, but more accessible. The closer you are to the main attraction on stage, the better the view. Bishop TD Jakes, world-renowned author, preacher, teacher, businessman, and mentor to many, explained it this way: Think of the seating arrangements at a concert or theater show. You know the front row seats are prime seating. The seating is usually arranged in tiers—the front row, orchestra seating, middle seating, balcony seating, and the nosebleed seating. The closer you are to the front, the more valuable the seats. You have to think of your life that way too. Your front row is reserved for special people. Everyone does not get a seat in your front row.

The front rows are those seats that are closest to you. The middle seats are a little further back and of course, the nosebleed seats are much further back. That's how access to your life should be. Your circle of friends and family that have your best interests at heart, support you, and love you—they get access to your front row. Even Jesus had a front row. All the twelve disciples were his (one was even a traitor, Judas, but even he served a purpose). But Peter, James, and John were closest to him, in his front row, and shared more intimate moments with him, seeing him at his most vulnerable.

Your front row is so precious because these are people you can trust to be vulnerable with. They have access to you like no one else, so you need to be selective and careful about whom you allow to have that type of access.

Again, Bishop TD Jakes explained it best in his teachings on "Confidants, Constituents, and Comrades." He said that confidants are those people closest to you—your front row—that you can give close access to; that you can be vulnerable with; that you can trust because you know they love you and you love them. They have your best interests at heart, and their loyalty is not in question.

Constituents are people that hitch their wagon to you so you can help get them to a personal or professional goal of their own, or because they believe their association with you can further their cause. If someone else comes along that they believe can get them there faster, they will drop you like a hot potato and move on. Don't expect loyalty from constituents. It's not their role, and your trust will be misplaced.

Now comrades are people that can come together for a common goal, but they can be total enemies or on opposite sides. Comrades come together to defeat a common enemy. This happens all the time in wars, when two or more countries come together against another country. They achieve a common goal and then the alliance is over, until the next time.

The problem occurs when you put people in the wrong category. For example, considering constituents as confidants, or comrades as confidants. It's a recipe for disappointment and hurt feelings every time, when you expect someone to be what they are not designed to be in a particular role.

Again, this was yet another hard-learned lesson. I would put constituents in the confidant category in my life and expect loyalty and friendship, and of course I would be disappointed. One thing about me is, loyalty and trust are huge. Once either is broken or betrayed, I can forgive and I can be cordial and kind, but the relationship will never be the same. As my mom used to say, "I'll feed you with a long-handled spoon." I'll be nice to you, but you won't get close to me again. I was a master at "long-handled spoon" dealings when I was younger. I would hold a grudge like nobody's business. If you crossed me, you were dead to me. Harsh, I know, but true. I'm just being honest.

Thankfully, I got over that and now categorize properly. Now I've learned to put people in the right place in my life—in the right row, that is—and not expect out of them what they are not meant to give or receive. Don't expect loyalty from constituents, and definitely not from comrades, and they don't get a seat in your front row.

When I first started building my business, I would get so close with my business partners because we were in the trenches working together, and some would become like family. I would mistakenly put some of them (constituents) in the confidant category and be significantly let down because they would come and go, as they were only there for a season or a reason, not a lifetime. They were there for a specific purpose—to build a business, make network connections, grow their contacts to use for other endeavors, etc. Now I was blessed in that some of my partners truly became family, good friends, and confidants.

I won't take too much time on comrades. You've heard the old adage, "Keep your friends close and your enemies closer." Well, that does *not* apply here! I get the meaning behind it, where you want to keep an eye on your enemies so they can't get close and hurt you, but enemies (a.k.a. comrades) do not get a seat close to you in your front row—or middle row, for that matter. You deal with comrades for a specific purpose, if you must, and for a finite period of time. They may not like you or you them. You don't have to like each other to get a job done. You may come together for a specific reason to defeat a common cause, like cancer, or to win a war, and then go your separate ways.

Now onto my favorite, confidants. They are the absolute best and the lifeblood in your relationships. They are life to you and help keep you going through the difficult times and are there to share and rejoice with you in the good times. This is your circle. This is your tribe, your circle of trust, people with whom you can laugh, spend time, cry, share, and be vulnerable and transparent. Primo front-row seating!

These seats or places in your life definitely are not for everyone and are not given lightly. They have much more value, so choose wisely whom you allow to sit in them and have that up-close access to you. These front-row seats are reserved for the closest and dearest people in your life. When you find and have that right circle and have the right people in your front row, it's absolutely priceless, and you wouldn't trade anything in the world for them. Hold onto them for dear life, as they are few and far between.

Your misstep might be your next step to success.

All Things Work Together for Good.
~ Romans 8:28, KJV

I still remember years ago, in my twenties, crying in the bathroom stall at work, trying to get my face together so I could walk out and not look like I had been crying. I had made one of the worst (honest) mistakes at work while troubleshooting an equipment failure. I had to send some diagnostic logs to the vendor, but little did I know, I had included in the logs some proprietary information that I had no idea was there and should not have been faxed. The incident was reported, and I was reprimanded and sent to another location—literally escorted out of the building—while the incident was investigated. I was absolutely mortified, embarrassed, and humiliated to say the least!

It took every ounce of strength not to break down and cry in front of these people. I had to put my game face on. It brings tears to my eyes just thinking about it now.

When I did finally come out of the stall, I gathered my things and left, escorted. My supervisor cried too. So much for trying to keep my game face on. My eyes were red, and everyone could tell I had been crying. Mostly, I was just scared because it was a contract job, and I was a single mom with three small kids, and I did not know if I was going to lose my job.

Well, the investigation concluded successfully. It was determined that I made an honest mistake with no malicious intent, and after eight months, I was offered my job back at the original location. Whew! That was one of the worst incidents of my life.

However, during the time at the temporary location, some great things happened. I made some amazing contacts, coworkers, and even met my future husband. Those contacts led to an official federal government job, no longer contracting, which offered the stability I needed as a single mom of three.

Sometimes what you think is the worst thing to happen to you can be a setup for success. Your perceived setback can actually be a setup to greater blessings and promotions. Your misstep might be your next step to success.

I love that scripture in Romans 8:28, KJV: "All things work together for good." It's basically saying that whatever the situation, good or bad, God can use it to work out for your good. All things, not some things, not just the good things, but all things work together for your good. It does not always feel that way, especially when you're going through a tough time. When you're doubting yourself or doubting your decisions, it can be hard to remember that God can turn those situations around for your good and in your favor.

That's where faith and trust come in. It's easy to trust when everything is going well. The real test and need for faith and trust is when it seems like everything is going wrong. When all hell's breaking loose: your spouse is sick, your kids are acting up, a divorce, or even a pandemic! This is also why it's important to have the right people in your front row as confidants that can speak life and affirming words back to you when you're going through those difficult times.

The situation could be teaching you or strengthening your faith or introducing you to new talents, skills, and strength you never knew you had that were already in you just waiting to be discovered. You'll find that you're stronger than you thought you were or gave yourself credit for.

Have you ever heard the term *failing forward*? Acclaimed author and leadership coach John Maxwell wrote an entire book about it. Adding *forward* to the word *failing* changes the whole concept of failing. Of course, no one likes to fail, but in reality, it's going to happen, because we are human. Failing forward means that even though you may view the situation as a failure, you don't go backwards. You move forward. You don't stay down; you rise up and let the experience make you greater as you learn from it and apply those lessons learned to propel you forward to your next level. So in that sense, was it really a failure? I'd venture to say no.

I heard a gentleman say that he doesn't fail, he learns. Now that's the right attitude! That's how you turn lemons into lemonade. It's turning a bad situation into a good one.

Years ago, in another job, I was getting ready for a huge inspection. I spent months preparing for it, working with multiple teams, ensuring everything was right, but then I failed the inspection. I was devastated! Again, I was sitting at work with my game face on trying to keep it together and not cry in front of anyone.

When I told my brother about the situation, he said, "Great! You're going to learn more from your failures than your successes." He told me I had not failed enough. I thought he was absolutely crazy! As I got older, I realized I had never really taken risks, so I was not used to failure; not that you want to fail at work. However, I had played it so safe to minimize failures, to the maximum extent possible, that I also did not win either. No risk, no reward.

To circle back to the inspection, I did pass the reinspection, but the experience made me dig in more, learn more, and it made me stronger and better the next time around. Again, what appears to be a misstep can actually be your next step to success—and a better you.

Driven

My husband says I'm just driven. When I make my mind up to do something, it is going to get done. I'm all in.

If it's worth your time, then it should be worth your effort, or you're just wasting time. I love words and I love the synonyms for *driven*. *Driven* means ambitious, focused, motivated, and determined. That's me, all day, every day. Your *why* should drive you. I've heard it said, "Your why should make you cry." If your why is not big enough, it won't drive you during the hard times, during the rough times, during the times when you don't feel like it, or during the times when it's easier to quit.

Sometimes you have to peel back the layers of the onion to get to your real why. People say they are driven by money, but it's not the money, it's what the money will accomplish: getting out of debt, financial freedom, retiring without having to go back to work or get a second job, having more than enough, being able to give without robbing Peter to pay Paul, or engaging in philanthropy. Studies have shown that money alone has a short-term impact on incentive because as soon as it's gone, it loses its effect and people forget about it.

It could be about time freedom. What does that mean to you? To me, it means I can see my adult children and family anytime I want, and I can stay as long as I want (with their approval, of course), not just the weekend or over a long weekend. It means I can wake up when I finish sleeping or I can go to bed when I'm tired, not because the alarm clock goes off at 5:00 a.m. so I can get up by 6:00 a.m. to sit in two hours of traffic roundtrip to go to work. Time freedom is working from anywhere I want and when I want, even from the beach. Sitting in traffic and having to ask for time off is the opposite of time freedom.

My why is creating a legacy for my children and my family, where we all have options to do what we want. I want to leave a legacy for my children and family that lives beyond me. Legacy, as most people understand it, is money, and for some people, it is time. I agree that legacy is money and time, but I would like to add another key ingredient: teaching your children and family members how to run a business and how to handle money. When we teach our children, our legacy will continue beyond us and break the generational cycle of poverty or having "just enough." We are called to live in abundance; more than enough, not just enough. So let your drive . . . drive you to some amazing places to accomplish some amazing things. Your dreams deserve for you to show up and give it your all.

Money and time are tools to enable so many other things. So again, your why has to drive you and be bigger than you.

I did some soul-searching after thinking about what my husband said about my being driven. I had to peel back the layers of the onion to get to the reason why I'm so driven. I'm definitely driven by my personal why. Peeling back those layers, I realized my drive stemmed from a desire for stability and to never experience lack again.

Growing up, it was kind of unstable. We moved around a lot. By the time I graduated, my family and I had moved eight different times; and we were not even a military family then. My mom got sick, and my dad was not well either, so my brother and I had to live with relatives for a while. Before we moved in with them, there were times when the electricity was turned off when my mom was sick. Although we had different family members who took us in, loved us, and did the best they could, we were still bounced around.

I always felt like a burden, or like I just didn't belong or didn't have a home of my own. Wherever I was, it wasn't my home or my room. It was someone else's.

When my uncle and aunt took us in, I did eventually find some stability, but in the back of my mind, I always felt like a burden, or wondering when something was going to happen, or when the other shoe would drop. I knew taking us in was a big responsibility, so I did not want to add the financial burden of college on them as well. I didn't have anyone in my corner talking about college, scholarships, or financial aid. I didn't want to be a burden after high school, so I chose the military.

It wound up being a wonderful decision. It gave me a good foundation, a solid career choice, college money, and skills, and I met some great people. It also set me up for a great civilian career through drive, determination, grace, and opportunities, and I am forever grateful.

The military gave me direction and a great start in life, but I didn't feel like I had options, and I wanted my kids to have options. I never wanted my children to experience instability, not having security or a place to call a home of their own. That drove me for years to ensure I created a stable and safe environment for them and for the most part, we did not experience any significant lack. That's not to say we didn't have some uncomfortable times, but God always made a way and provided.

I always made sure I had a plan A, B, and C. That still drives me today. I never depend on a single source of income; I'm always looking to create multiple income streams. I'm no longer in survival mode. I realized that surviving is not thriving. I want to have more than enough, not just enough. I want to be able to give, to invest, and to be a blessing whenever I see or hear about a need.

So let your drive drive you to some amazing places to accomplish some amazing things. Your dreams are worth it and deserve for you to show up and give it your all. You've got this. Let's get it!

Movement Step, Action Step

Identify what you are passionate about: travel, health and wellness, writing, real estate, counseling? Next, reach out to someone in that field with proven results to see how to get started. Request coaching and accountability in that area. Take a course, go to a presentation, and start that business. You can do it! It starts with that first step, that first decision.

From Ashes is Born a Rose

Mary Adams

Imagine being married for twenty-one years but still being lonely.

Imagine feeling like you have a brick wall built around you, and you are screaming from the inside as loud as you can, but no one can hear you.

Imagine having to bend, twist, and contort yourself into a pretzel to stroke someone else's ego to make them happy while they don't have a concern in the world regarding what makes you happy.

I did not have to imagine these scenarios because that was the life I lived for fifteen years. I became adept at covering up just how unhappy I was. I would put a smile on my face when out with family or friends. I would make excuses for him when he did not go to a family dinner or come for a holiday or attend an outing with me. Making excuses for his absence became par for the course.

When people hear the phrase *domestic violence*, the scene playing in their minds may be reminiscent of Ike and Tina Turner, where Ike is beating Tina black and blue, and Tina is left with battle scars of bruises and eyes swollen shut, or broken bones.

That was not my reality, but I still experienced domestic violence. My reality was being torn down by words, mental and verbal abuse, which can hurt so much more than the physical. The bruises and the bones will heal, but the words stay with you and leave you questioning yourself and wondering if everyone you come into contact with feels the same way your antagonist does. You are always on edge, taking each step so gingerly and in fear of it being the wrong step, because someone put in your mind that you are less than, you are not capable, you are not smart enough, you aren't pretty enough, you aren't, you won't, you can't…every outcome being negative. That was my reality. But in the end, I flipped the script and now I can, I will, I do. I AM enough. This is my story.

I knew I was unhappy in the marriage, but I did not realize *how* unhappy I was until it was over. Until I was able to start peeling back the onion and rediscovering who I was. I had bent over backwards trying to be flexible and compromised on things I felt strongly about so I would not have to spend hours debating with someone when I knew I would never win in the end. I lost touch with myself and what made me happy because I had compromised myself for so long that I didn't even recognize the person reflected back at me in the mirror.

To have every thought or idea I had criticized by the person that was supposed to love me for better or for worse was so hurtful. I am college-educated, career-oriented, and a hard worker who got through fifty-two years of life. I was so angry and disappointed all of the time. I was taking care of him financially and raising our daughter, but being told that I could not think on my own; that I was a horrible mother; that I lied and was a thief. He said whatever he had to in order to tear me down emotionally. He broke me down to the point that I no longer had a voice. I could no longer battle with him because I had lost so much already.

I was trapped. I was a bird in a cage that wanted to fly but my wings were clipped. Deep down was the smallest voice: *You have to get out of this marriage. You deserve happiness. You and your daughter deserve better than this.* It was time for me to fly.

I formulated a plan, my exit strategy. I took out a loan from my employer-sponsored TSA (Tax Sheltered Annuity) plan to pay off some debt and get our daughter into college. Paying off this debt significantly improved my credit score. I worked all the overtime that was available from my full-time job to pay off some smaller debts. Then I looked at my monthly household budget and started cutting corners on unnecessary spending and figuring out how to reduce other bills. I was also able to refinance my vehicle, since my credit score had improved, to save an additional $75 per month on my car note. These financial decisions would ensure that when the time came to leave the marriage, I would be ready.

For I know the plans I have for you, declares the Lord,
plans to prosper you, and not to harm you,
plans to give you hope and a future.
~ Jeremiah 29:11, NIV

The Beginning

The only real male role model I had when I was a child was my grandfather, because my father was an absentee dad. While my father lived in our household until I was eleven years old, he chose not to participate much in my or my brother's life. He worked the graveyard shift, so he slept all day. The only time my brother and I came into contact with our father, for the most part, was at dinner. But even then, he sat in the dining room while we ate in the kitchen, and he had a newspaper in front of him to read while he ate his dinner, so all we saw was the back of a newspaper.

My mother, my brother, and I spent a lot of time at our grandparents' house when I was growing up. Before my grandfather was forced to retire due to an on-the-job injury, he was a dedicated employee and always worked a double shift at Bethlehem Steel. Looking back, between my grandfather and my mother, this is where I got my strong work ethic. My mother never missed a day, even when she was sick. And then when she got home, she would cook dinner and then spend the rest of the night cleaning the house.

Our grandfather always lectured my brother and me about the importance of getting an education and having a strong work ethic. But he also lectured me about my weight. I remember when I was between the ages of eight and ten, my grandfather was always asking me to get on the scale. He told me I was too pudgy or chunky, or too big around the middle. He never used the word fat, but I knew what he meant.

When I was in my twenties, my grandfather was hospitalized, and he told me that he did not like me. He said it was because I pulled away from him one Sunday when we were walking home from church when I was about five years old. There was a field that separated my grandparents' home from the church that we would walk across each Sunday to go to church. On this particular Sunday, when we were walking home, I pulled away from him and clung to my mother, and he never liked me from that day forward.

I do not recall this event, but clearly, he did. Maybe this was why he would pick on me about my weight, even as a child. Perhaps this is where my lack of self-esteem began.

So, when I was about one or two years into my relationship with my then boyfriend and he started badgering me about my weight, it all seemed normal, because it was what I had experienced as a child.

The Middle

We started dating in the late eighties, when I was twenty years old and he was twenty-seven. My mother was unhappy with the relationship because he was Black. Interracial relationships were not as commonplace as they are now, and she thought I would have issues. I always had Black friends and did not see a problem with dating someone of another race. My mother did not approve, so when I was twenty-one, I decided to move into my own apartment. That way, he and I would have our own space to get together.

I worked three jobs to pay the bills, but I was happy and excited to be on my own. I should have realized then that there was a problem. I was working three jobs—one full-time job in the corporate world, and two part-time jobs, one in a gym teaching aerobics several times a week, and a weekend job in a convenience store. I was working seven days a week so I could have an apartment where we could freely see one another, and he did not offer any financial assistance.

We had a normal courtship. We hung out with friends, went to the movies, went out to dinner, went out for drinks, and had friends over to my apartment to play cards. Then, about two years into our relationship, I started picking up a few pounds. I was working three jobs since I got the apartment, and no longer had the time I previously had to go to the gym to work out. When I started gaining a little weight, it caused some friction in the relationship. I just shrugged it off. I joined Weight Watchers, I lost the weight, and life continued. But whenever he felt that I was gaining weight, that conversation would rear its ugly head again.

Four years into the relationship, I lost my corporate job due to downsizing. I decided to take the voluntary separation and the twelve-month severance package. I used the money to go back to school and finish my associate degree. Of course, this meant giving up my apartment and moving back in with my mother. I decided I had had enough of the relationship and the arguing about my weight, so I broke it off. We remained friends, and occasionally saw each other socially.

Fast-forward two years, and his best friend—whom I loved dearly—was murdered. This grief brought us back together. We slowly started to mend our relationship and got back together. I graduated with my associate's degree and took another corporate job with a law firm, and was very happy starting my career in my field of study. The next few years were good. We went out with friends, went out on dates to dinner and the movies. We visited a friend who had moved to San Diego. There was an occasional mention of my weight, but it was never a point of contention.

In 1997, we got engaged, and were married in 1999. Leading up to our wedding, I was spending a lot of time at the gym slimming down for the wedding. I was never going to be a size eight; I don't have that petite body type, but I wanted to look good.

We were married in May 1999 and moved into our own home in December 1999. A little more than a year later, he quit his job without having another job lined up and without telling me he was going to quit. This is also when I noticed that he was drinking more and hanging out with friends more to drink. I would come home to an empty house because he was out with friends. Or I would come home, and he was already in bed asleep. The loneliness began.

Again, I took on a part-time job, along with working my full-time corporate job, to make sure we could make ends meet. He was unemployed for about six months. Again, my strong work ethic took over and I did what it took to keep the household functioning.

Then I got pregnant. I was overjoyed! He was very happy too but wondered how we were going to be able to afford a baby. I was still working at my part-time job, and he started working again. I said we would find a way. I am a hard worker, and always found a way when I wanted or needed something. I was thirty-three and ready for a baby and a family. But after a few months, it became too taxing for me to be pregnant and hold down two jobs. So, since he was working full-time, I quit my part-time job.

He came to every single one of my prenatal appointments and ultrasounds. He was becoming the model husband and prospective father. He would talk about how excited he was to become a father and how involved he would be in their life. He would be at every sporting event, recital, school event, you name it. He told me that when he was growing up, his father did not attend many of his sporting events. Therefore, he knew how important it would be to our future child to attend such events.

But that was not to be; it was all just words. Sure, he came to a few events, but much of the time, he would give excuses that he was too tired to come to the winter or spring concert, or the soccer game, or he had to work. There was always an excuse, and our daughter was so disappointed. But I would put a positive spin on it, even though I knew she probably didn't buy a word I was saying.

Just as he had come to each of my prenatal appointments, he came to every one of our daughter's early pediatrician appointments. I was trying to breastfeed, but my body was not producing enough milk for her, so she was losing weight. It got to the point that we had to go for a weight check every other day for the first few weeks of her life. The doctor told us that losing half an ounce of weight when you weigh only seven pounds is a lot, and if I did not switch her to formula, she would have to be admitted to the hospital for dehydration. Of course, I did not want that to happen, so I supplemented every other feeding with formula. She became a much happier baby and started picking up weight, so I made the tough decision to completely switch to formula, since breastfeeding was just too difficult.

At nearly every doctor's appointment, she was off the charts, not only for weight, but also for height. Our daughter was very tall and stood heads above the other children her age. So, since she was always in the ninety-fifth percentile for height and weight, her father started asking the doctor if she was going to be overweight. This started at the tender age of one or two years old. What was it with this guy and weight?

His comments got progressively worse the older our daughter got. He would tell the pediatrician to look at me and my issues with weight and that I must be overfeeding our daughter. I was so embarrassed that I could not even respond in front of the doctor when he made these comments.

The doctor and I both told him that it was baby fat, and that once she became more active, the weight would come off. The doctor showed him a picture of her own daughter at around the same age—with rolls and rolls of baby fat—and then showed us a picture of her a few years older, and she had slimmed down. By the looks she was giving him, she too must have felt that this was such a strange conversation to be having when our daughter was only a few years old.

We had this conversation at every annual pediatrician visit. I was embarrassed and extremely uncomfortable at each visit because he made me feel so inadequate as a parent. He blamed me, as the caregiver, because I was the one preparing the meals and feeding her. However, he never considered that he would take her to McDonald's and get her chicken nuggets, a cheeseburger, and French fries. He also would not allow her to play outside. We constantly argued about this.

On top of that, he started comparing my parenting to that of a Black mother, stating that a Black mother would never let her child say or do things that I allowed our daughter to do or say. We had a good daughter who was never in any trouble. She got excellent grades, and she was involved in Girl Scouts, soccer, and basketball, so I did not understand why he was so hard on her all the time.

Then I was upset with him because he drank beer every day and was asking his young child to bring him a beer from the refrigerator. This became a point of contention. I was trying so hard to mold us into this family unit that I did not have as a child because my parents had divorced, and I was beginning to compromise what I thought was right to give our daughter a two-parent household.

He was a wordsmith and a spin doctor. At the time, I did not realize he was trying to break me down emotionally and mentally with verbal abuse. Everything was a catch-22. If I said one thing he would spin it the other way, and vice versa. There was never any winning with him. He would debate everything to death, until I just acquiesced to whatever he said because I would get tired of arguing with him or debating. It was draining. I started to live my life with the "don't poke the bear" mentality. But that never seemed to work either. I literally did not have peace, even in my own home.

When our daughter got older and we would return to our home after a day out, she said that her whole body would tense up when we came around the corner and saw his car parked in front of the house, because you just never knew what would be waiting for you on the other side of the door. But when we came around the corner and his car was not there, her whole body would relax. I felt exactly the same way. Living like that was exhausting.

He was also extremely charming and funny, and there were periods of time when I was happy. But then one wrong look or comment, or I did not live up to an expectation that he had, and it would all go south again. I don't want it to seem all doom and gloom, because there would be days at a time when life was good. He would be joking and smiling, and we would have a good time.

Then, in our daughter's last two years of high school, he quit three different jobs, all without having another job lined up. Every time he quit a job, the reason was the same—the management was racist, or it was a hostile work environment. He was always the victim. Someone else was always to blame. "The management is horrible. They don't know what they are doing. I have been in the hospitality business for twenty-five-plus years, so I know how to do it." The excuses went on and on.

During our daughter's senior year of high school, I made the decision that I could not live like this anymore. I deserve better. I cannot be with someone who is verbally abusive to me, especially when I am the only one that has ever stood beside him. I could no longer stand for someone that would quit their job at the drop of a hat when we had a daughter in college. I could no longer take someone who was not contributing to the household financially, but always made sure they had money for their cigarettes, beer, scotch, and marijuana.

I could no longer be in a relationship with someone who clearly did not love me. I felt I was being taken advantage of and being taken for granted. I knew this person, whom I had been with for thirty years, was not going to change, and that he had deep-rooted issues I could not resolve for him. It was not my job to take care of him. He needed to deal with the hurts he had from childhood. He had to man up and decide to get help on his own. I was no longer going to allow him to make our daughter and me his punching bags to take all his hurts out on.

This is when I formulated my exit strategy.

In addition to making a financial plan, I began doing things I had been neglecting and that would make me happier individually. I began to travel. I joined a book club. I got a keto coach and started losing weight (for me), and I started walking a few times a week with a good friend.

One friend knew I enjoyed reading and was restarting her book club. She invited me to join, and it was one of the best decisions I made. She didn't know at the time, but she threw me a lifeline. It was a lifeline because it was a diverse group of women, and there was no drama.

But we did not just talk about the book-of-the-month selection, we also talked about life. About all of its ups and downs. About marriage, children, school, sex, life events, politics, you name it.

At these book club talks, I would see and hear examples of what a good marriage and family really looked like, and it wasn't mine. During these book club get-togethers, I began to see just how out of whack my marriage was. But it also gave me what I needed at the time, which was emotional support, even if the ladies in the book club didn't know it. It was my outlet, my time to be myself. My time to laugh. My time to bond with people who cared about me. My time to be around people who did not judge me or knock me down. I never missed a book club talk (and still don't). In fact, those book club meetings made me stronger. I could feel it from the inside out.

We decided to go on an annual retreat. The first year, we travelled to Florida, and the second year, we went to Deep Creek Lake in the mountains of western Maryland. Each trip was so much fun and relaxing. It was a time to be myself and let my guard down. I was enjoying life again.

I became close to another book club member while we worked together planning our first annual retreat. We started walking together several times a week. Walking was helping me get stronger, physically and mentally. We had spirited conversations during these walks, and she could tell I was unhappy. I began to open up to her, and I started to dismantle the brick wall I had built around myself, brick by brick, walk by walk. To have a sounding board in someone that I trusted—who had gone through divorce herself—was so eye-opening. She helped me dig deep inside myself and see how unsatisfying this relationship was, and how I was putting my happiness on the back burner and not living the life I deserved.

My friend and I traveled to Dallas together and attended Oprah's 2020 Vision Tour. During this one-day workshop, Oprah touched on so many topics that hit me right to my core and solidified that the choices I had been making were the right ones. The year 2020 was my year for change in so many areas: getting fit, eating healthy, losing weight, getting out of a bad marriage, doing activities that made me happier, and spending more time with friends.

Then my husband started criticizing me about going to each book club meeting, saying I was only going because food was involved. Of course the food was good; we always picked the best restaurants to go to. But it wasn't that. It was the camaraderie, the mutual trust and friendship among people who spent a lot of time together. I needed that time.

When he saw that I was becoming happier because I was doing things for myself, of course he started to tear me down. He said I thought I was "all that" because I had a good job and could work from home. I told him that I worked hard to get to where I was and that I would not allow him to be condescending to me anymore. If he was so unhappy, he could leave. But he knew that he couldn't, because he had quit several jobs and was struggling financially.

Since he could see that he could no longer tear me down because I had become happier, working on myself, he turned his attention to tearing our daughter down, again by fat-shaming her. On our four-hour drive to her college to move her into her dorm, he kept telling her that she would be the fattest freshman checking into the dorm, and how did that make her feel? This was supposed to be such an exciting time for her—and for us as parents—and here he was making it the most miserable. I hated him for what he was doing. He made the whole weekend horrible.

When our daughter came home from college for Christmas break, the whole focus was on her and how she had gained the typical "Freshman 15." She's in school, away from home, away from family and friends, trying to adjust to life away from home and having to eat what is available in the dining hall. He didn't understand, nor did he care to.

Everything escalated when she came home for spring break. Our daughter saw how well I was doing on keto with my weight loss. She asked if she could do it with me during spring break so she could follow the program and see if it would be something she could easily do while she was at college. Of course, I was excited that she wanted to do it with me and that we could also go to the gym together.

He started arguing, asking what good would one week do when she would gain it all back when she returned to school. What good would going to the gym do if she didn't have a gym membership when she returned to school? He was always putting down any effort our daughter made at doing anything.

Then, about three days into her break, he started saying that he was going to kill me and then kill himself. He continued asking me, "What parent does everything they can to lose weight but is just watching their child gain weight or doing nothing to help their child lose weight?" At that time, I was getting close to having lost forty-five pounds. When he got on a roll, he could talk, yell, and shout for hours at a time. There was no talking to him.

I had formulated my exit plan and I was coming close to being able to make my move to get out of this crappy marriage. Then, two days later, everything flipped on its head, and my plan for getting out of this marriage that was riddled with verbal abuse moved at warp speed.

The End

I heard his heavy footsteps come into the house around 7:30 p.m. I heard him cursing under his breath. I was working and had thirty minutes left of my work shift. My whole body got tense because, from the sound of his footsteps and him mumbling expletives under his breath, I knew the rest of the evening was not going to go well.

His steps thundered up the stairs to the third level of the house, to our daughter's bedroom, where he began shouting at her, "I am going to kill your mother, and then I am going to kill myself!" He was yelling that at her, over and over again. I was two floors below them and could hear every word. Terror shot from my toes all the way out to my fingertips. He had never exploded like this before, least of all at our daughter.

I am a work-from-home agent with a health insurance company, and I was on the phone with a member. I was trying to hurry up and get this member off the phone, when the next thing I heard was him running down the stairs to confront me. My body tensed up even more. He stood over me, yelling that he was going to kill me. I kept having to mute the phone so the member I was speaking with would not hear what was going on.

I tried to tell my husband that I was on a work call and that he would have to wait ten more minutes until I got off and then I could discuss with him whatever his issue was at that moment. He kept yelling that he did not care that I was on the phone, and he did not care what happened to my job. He was going to kill me and then himself. I don't know what I said next because he went back upstairs to our daughter's room and started yelling at her again.

The next thing I knew, she was running down the stairs to me and he was yelling behind her that she'd better not come downstairs. By the time she reached me, she was visibly upset and crying, and her face was red. My daughter said we had to go, but I was still trying to wrap up this call with the same member. We heard my husband stop in the kitchen and the next thing we knew he was coming down the stairs, and when he reached the bottom of the staircase where my office desk was, he was carrying the largest butcher's knife we owned, pointing it at the two of us. I was terrified. My whole life was flashing before my eyes.

I was sitting down, my daughter was standing behind me, and he was standing about two feet away from me with his arm outstretched, threatening us with this large butcher knife. I didn't know what to do.

Finally, I was able to get this member off the phone. I kept asking my husband to put down the knife and he refused. Because he was standing over me and I was between him and my daughter, I had nowhere to go, and I was not certain as to what my next move would be.

I took a chance and tried to grab the knife out of his hand when he took his eyes off me to look at our daughter. He yelled at me not to touch him.

In that split second, he changed position and I was able to jump up and behind my desk chair to create a barrier between us, and then I pushed our daughter behind me so she was further away from him. At all costs, I was going to protect my daughter. I yelled at her to run out the back door, which was in the opposite direction of him, and to call 911. My daughter would not leave me; she wanted to protect me, no matter how many times I kept telling her to run out the back door and call 911.

Because everything was happening so fast, I forgot that my cell phone was on my desk. I grabbed it and dialed 911. He dropped the knife to his side and said that I did not have to call 911, that he would put the knife up, and he went back upstairs.

While I was on the phone with 911, giving our address and all the details of what was going on, I kept hearing him going in and out of our front door, from outside to inside and then back again. I did not know if he planned on leaving before the police arrived, so I gave a description of his car and the tag number.

The 911 dispatcher told me to stay in the basement until the police arrived. I did not hear any movement from upstairs, so I tiptoed up the stairs. I could see the reflection of the police lights from the clock that was at the top of the staircase. When I looked out the door, there were four patrol cars out front, and my husband was being arrested. He kept yelling at the police officers that were handcuffing him, "What am I being arrested for?" I was thinking, *Are you kidding me? You don't even comprehend why you are being arrested?*

Two police officers came inside after he was arrested and took my statement. Then the female police officer stayed and gave me a ten-question domestic violence questionnaire. The survey was eye-opening.

Once we completed it, she said that I scored very high for being in extreme danger and potentially dead right now. She provided me with information on how to file a protective order, and what his next steps would be after being arrested. Since it was a Friday night, she said most likely he would be in jail all weekend and would go before the commissioner on Monday for a bail review. My daughter and I went to the district court to file for a protective order, which the commissioner granted.

Now the ball was in my court, and I was going to make the rules and take back my life. This was my opportunity. I had a temporary protective order, and he was in jail, at least until Monday, when he would go before the commissioner, who would decide if he would remain in jail until his preliminary hearing.

The following morning, I went to our bank and closed out our joint checking account, then opened an account in my name only. I was not giving him the opportunity, if he got out on Monday, of going to the bank and clearing out the money in our account.

On Monday, I went to the courthouse in Towson and obtained the 911 transcript and provided that to the DOVE program that provides free legal services and counseling services to domestic violence victims. I also put in a request for the police report.

On Tuesday, I had the locks changed on the doors to our home, and I consulted with a family law attorney on the process of filing a separation agreement and divorce. I decided to retain his services and we discussed the terms of the separation. All I wanted was my house.

About two weeks after meeting with the attorney, my husband was served the separation agreement. About two weeks later, he sent my attorney an email, basically stating that he would not be signing the separation agreement because he could not afford an attorney, and he could not sign something that he did not understand. He also stated that while the divorce was important, it was more urgent for him to hire an attorney for the criminal charges, for which he did not have the funds. Once again, he was making himself the victim.

I was not falling for it. My attorney advised that we could proceed with an absolute divorce based upon cruelty and excessively vicious conduct.

When we went back to court for the final protective order hearing in late May 2020, it was granted for an entire year; he was also served with the divorce. He would have thirty days to respond to contest anything he disagreed with, or to make a counteroffer.

In his counteroffer, he alleged that I was the one who was cruel in the marriage because I was stealing money from him. I managed the household budget and because I did not allocate funds the way he wanted them to be allocated, he was accusing me of stealing from him, although he had opened his own account nearly twelve years ago and all household finances were being paid out of our joint account that he contributed no funds to. When he paid a bill, he would either pay out of his account or he would give me cash. How is this stealing?

He also alleged that I was cruel because I caused our daughter to be overweight, which gave him cause for concern for her overall health, and that I was the root cause of her becoming emotionally separated from him.

We submitted a discovery request to his attorney, questioning what documents he would be using to prove these allegations. Once again, being the narcissist that he is, he was making himself the victim and looking for someone to blame for all the hurt he had caused. We both wanted the same outcome, so why was he making this uglier and more drawn out than it needed to be?

The last few months have been difficult, dealing with the aftermath of what happened. But on the other hand, they have been the best few months in the last 15 years, because I have had peace in my house, and I have not had to tiptoe around on eggshells in my own home and wonder when the other shoe is going to drop, or what he is upset about now.

I am rediscovering Mary and what makes me happy. Remember the Mary that was trapped in a cage that was unable to fly? I have found my wings again. I have found my voice. I am learning what makes me happy, one day at a time.

I was not given permission to plant flowers, so one weekend, I planted flowers in the garden and discovered that I enjoy the serenity of planting flowers and watching them blossom. I look forward to watering my flowers every day and after a month, getting excited to see that they are finally starting to bloom.

I went hiking for the first time with friends in the early spring and loved it. I enjoyed being out in nature, and the peace and the sounds of the woods and seeing the waterfall and running water. It was so relaxing. I have been one time since then and enjoyed it just as much.

I am enjoying sitting out on both of my decks that I have redecorated, just reading and listening to music while savoring a glass of wine.

I have joined three other book clubs: Oprah's Book Club; Reese Witherspoon's Book Club; and the Barnes & Noble Book Club. I enjoy the online communication with other readers and the interviews with the authors.

I did a virtual 5K with the Baltimore Women's Classic. I finished in fifty-seven minutes and twenty-three seconds. My goal was to finish in less than one hour and I did it! Since then, I have downloaded the Couch to 5K app, and it promises to have me running a 5K in nine weeks. At the time of this writing, I am on Week 7 of this nine-week journey to running. My goal, however, is not to be a runner but a slow jogger, somewhere between walking and running.

Even though the divorce is still pending, I have never been happier. I am sleeping better, I am down sixty-three pounds as of this writing, I am healthier, and I am looking forward to whatever the future holds for me.

The DOVE program provides free mental health services. About a month ago, I started having weekly sessions with a therapist to talk through all of the feelings I am having, everything I have been through and will go through, to help me sort through my feelings and start to have a more positive outlook on life. This has helped me tremendously.

Just like I dismantled the wall I built brick by brick, to get to the core of Mary and who she is, I am now taking the time to focus on myself. I am rebuilding the wall by starting with the foundation of who I am and what makes me happy, truly happy, and brings joy and purpose to my life. Once the foundation is complete, I can add bricks to start building the house of Mary, where I will live and dwell. Then I will decide who and what gets my time and attention and whether they add to my life or not.

I am now excited for what the future may hold for me. I am FREE to live my life. I am looking forward to discovering what makes me happy and taking on new challenges and experiences. We get a finite amount of time on this Earth, I choose to surround myself from this point forward with those that will add to my life and be positive influences and help me grow and be all I can be. I do not know my final destination, but I am looking forward to taking this journey.

"From Ashes is Born a Rose"

"Breathe...Relax...Tell your truth. Today is the start to you helping a lot of people. This will not be the only day you're asked to speak on it. God bless. We're proud of you. This is a new you. Anytime a flower is blooming it has to break through hardened ground. Similarly, a butterfly breaking through the cocoon is the most difficult part of its life cycle. But, the process of breaking through the cocoon is what strengthens the wings enough for it to fly. It's necessary for it to fly. You're that butterfly today. Fly. All you went through made you stronger. This is only the beginning of you being a spokesperson for surviving domestic violence. You will be such a resource for women in the same position who don't know what to do. Let God have the control."

Jay, Johnathan Creekmur
Educator, Cousin, Husband, Father

Movement, Action Step:

If you or someone you know has left an abusive relationship, seek the help of a mental health therapist, a clergy member, or a domestic violence group, such as DOVE, to discuss how the relationship has affected you so you may move forward with your life. Know that it was not your fault.

Q &A
with the Authors

How did you all come together and decide to write the book? What's the backstory of how you came together?

Tracey

I decided to write this book because I spent my adult years seeking to empower, strengthen, and uplift women, so I wanted to use my chapter to speak to those topics. I'm often asked where my sense of confidence comes from, and my chapter sets the foundation for that.

Joie

A few years ago, I had a conversation with Tracey about writing a book for my daughter. I wanted her to have a resource to refer to for wisdom and guidance about life. I am passionate about connecting, cultivating, and maintaining healthy relationships with women. I hope my story about the relationships I have with women and my passion inspires my daughter, along with other women of all ages, to invest in healthy, woman-to-woman connections.

Deidra

I decided to share my story in a book because I'm passionate about helping entrepreneurs, especially women, take the leap of faith, get out of their own way, and start their entrepreneurial journey in business, avoiding many of the pitfalls that can hinder their success in business. I especially wanted to share the journey of who they find, the person that's already in them, along the way.

Mary

When we returned from our second annual book club retreat in January 2020, Tracey mentioned that all of us shared so many stories during our retreat that touched on so many different topics. She asked all of us in the book club if we would be interested in writing a book together in a collaborative format. I had always had an interest in writing a novel, but not a memoir. She set up a workshop with a writing coach she knew, and after a few sessions, it blossomed into deciding that I wanted to be a part of this group and that I had something to share that might help other women dealing with issues of domestic violence.

What did you learn about yourself through this collaboration?

Tracey

I learned that although I have a strong foundation and high self-esteem, I'm forever a work in progress. I learned the importance of remaining open to building new and healthy relationships with those around me. I learned that working on this book collaboration, especially during the pandemic, has shown me how truly powerful sisterhood and connections are to your mental health and living an authentic life.

Joie

During this collaboration, I learned that I could write a book with other women I did not know and that although our stories are different, we still have all experienced the joys and challenges of being human and being women. Very recently, I learned about the backgrounds and personalities of Mary and Deidra. My interaction with them has been mostly virtual. The fact that we have not met in person has not interfered with connecting.

Deidra

I learned that we all have a story—and many of them are similar—that need to be told. We have so many gifts, talents, and wisdom hidden in us as women that can offer guidance, healing, and strength to so many others. The different perspectives and adding a voice to those experiences and feelings was very therapeutic as well.

Mary

Once I looked back on what I had written to share my story, I realized that I had put myself on the back burner for so long trying to satisfy someone else that I forgot about myself. I have learned to never take myself for granted; that my happiness matters; that I am important. That I need to take time to check in with myself. That I am giving myself the freedom to try new things; if I don't like it, at least I tried and I can move on to something else that does bring joy to my life.

About the Authors

Tracey Lanier Thompson, known as Coach Tracey, was born in Jersey City, NJ, raised in the northwest suburbs of Baltimore County, MD, and currently resides there. She's married to her soulmate, Michael "Mike Ferg" Thompson, and they have two beautiful children. She enjoys reading, listening to music, and learning new things!

The bulk of Tracey's previous career was that of being a Paralegal and 15+ years with the Baltimore County Public School system. She holds numerous degrees and accolades. In addition to being a Professional Life Coach, through the International Coaching Federation (ICF), Certified Professional Life Coach, ACSTH (June 2015), she was awarded a Master of Arts in Teaching from Goucher College, Baltimore, MD (May 2000); a Bachelor of Science Degree in Criminal Justice from University of Baltimore, Baltimore, MD (December 1993), and an Associate of Arts Degree in Paralegal Studies from Stevenson University, Stevenson, MD (December 1991).

Coach Tracey touches lives through her daily work by providing women with skills in understanding the choices they face, the decisions they make, and the potential they have, but so often do not recognize.

As a Certified Life Coach, Tracey expresses her passion by helping others live and lead their BEST LIFE. Coach Tracey is motivated by helping individuals truly enjoy the life they live with purpose and happiness.

She lives her life authentically by coaching women to live a purposeful and happy life. She is the founder of A Circle for Sisters™ (ACFS), a company originally created in 1997, but officially reestablished in 2020. ACFS provides women with opportunities to feel safe and valued in order to live, learn, grow, and share their stories through authentic experiences.

FUN FACTS ABOUT COACH TRACEY

1. She can spend hours in a bookstore.
2. Her favorite things to do are read books and watch Lifetime movies.
3. She met her husband at an open mic night.
4. Traveling to Italy is on her bucket list!

Deidra Bass

Cybersecurity Expert |
Travelprenuer | Speaker | Coach

Deidra is an accomplished Cybersecurity Expert, Travel Professional, Lifestyle Architect, Speaker and Coach, empowering people all over the world and in multiple genres. She began her career in the Federal Government over 30 years ago, first in the United States Navy for 11 years and in Civil Service for over 20 years. She rose through the ranks quickly and became the 1st African American Female Chief Information Security Officer (CISO) for her organization, providing Cybersecurity governance, policy and risk management to ensure the protection of information and information systems.

Also known as "The Travelprenuer", Deidra has always had a passion for travel, having traveled throughout Europe, to Ireland, Athens, Mykonos, and Santorini, Greece; Dubai, France, Spain, and Italy, where even her youngest two children were born. Her eldest was born in the USA. This led her to launch Bass Travels, LLC, where she was able to combine her passion for travel with her drive for entrepreneurship. Her motto is, "creating Dreams and memories that last a lifetime...without breaking the bank." She has a team of dynamic people committed to helping her on this journey. In addition, she is releasing her first collaborative book with "A Circle for Sisters" and solo book to include a journal called "The Travel Bible", a journal to creatively document travel and adventures filled with inspiration along the way.

Deidra's Coaching includes pouring into entrepreneurs all over the world teaching them solid business practices, how to launch a business, and how to treat their business like a business and not a hobby.

Deidra has a passion for giving. Through her philanthropic giving she's an avid supporter of St. Judes, Feed The Children, and a variety of religious organizations to help spread the Gospel and care to those in need.

Deidra is a Certified Travel Professional, certified Cruise Line International Association (CLIA) Professional, IATAN Certified, Accredited Cruise Counsellor (ACC), and in the area of Cybersecurity, a Certified Information System Security Professional (CISSP).

Deidra is available for Conferences, Workshops, Panel Discussions, and Seminars.

Deidra is married to Kenneth Bass, one of her biggest supporters, and is also a real estate investor owning her own company, B&B Property Solutions Group, LLC, with her adult children!! Entrepreneurship runs in the family!!

Joie Nichele Hill

Joie Hill was born, educated and lives in Baltimore, Maryland. She graduated from Western High School, the oldest all-female public high school in the United States. She earned a Bachelor of Arts in Government and Public Policy from the University of Baltimore. Joie is a devoted mother, sister, aunt and friend. She has worked for the Federal Government for over 28 years. She is a member of the New Psalmist Baptist Church and enjoys spending time with family and friends, celebratory gatherings, traveling, dancing, going to festivals, watching CNN, meeting new people, walking and reading books.

Joie is a new entrepreneur and recently completed life coach training. She is passionate about sisterhood and values her relationships with women. As a true extrovert, her spirit is filled and her heart is warmed when she connects with, supports and mentors people. She especially enjoys watching the Baltimore Ravens play football.

Mary Adams

Mary is the mother of one daughter who is a junior in college. She has an Associate's degree in Paralegal Studies and is currently working as a Customer Service Representative for a leading health insurance company. Mary enjoys reading, gardening, hiking, walking and running, and participates in several book clubs. Mary has run in several 5K's and recently completed her first Mud Run. Mary is looking forward to continuing her training to participate in future runs. Since writing her chapter, Mary's divorce has been finalized and she has purchased a new home.

Mary is enjoying her new-found freedom and decorating her new home to her likeness.

Resources

Agrawal, Radha. Belong: Find Your People, Create Community & Live a More Connected Life. Workman Publishing, 2018.

Eker, T. Harv. Secrets of the Millionaire Mind: Mastering the Inner Game of Wealth. New York: HarperCollins, 2009.

Jackson Gandy, Debrena. *All The Joy You Can Stand: 101 Sacred Power Principles for Making Joy Real in Your Life.* New York: Three Rivers Press, 2000.

Jackson, Danielle Bayard. Give it a Rest: The Case for Tough-Love Friendships. RDE Publishing, 2019.

Nelson, Shasta. Frientimacy. Seal Press, 2016.

Nichols, Lisa and Janet Switzer. *Abundance Now: Amplify Your Life & Achieve Prosperity Today.* New York: Harper Collins, 2016.

Rhimes, Shonda. *Year of Yes: How to Dance It Out, Stand In the Sun and Be Your Own Person.*

Shefali, Tsabary. *A Radical Awakening: Turn Pain into Power, Embrace Your Truth, Live Free.* New York: HarperOne, 2021.

Williams, A.L. All You Can Do Is All You Can Do, but All You Can Do Is Enough! Thomas Nelson Publishers, 1988.

Yarnell, Mark, and Rene Reid Yarnell. Your First Year in Network Marketing: Overcome Your Fears, Experience Success, and Achieve Your Dreams! Prima Publishing, 1998.

New York: Simon & Schuster, 2015.

For common signs of abusive behavior go to www.thehotline.com or contact the National Domestic Violence Hotline at 800-799-SAFE (7233).

For a brief Domestic Violence Screening Quiz, go to psychcentral.com to help determine if you might need to see a mental health or other social service professional to help you successfully deal with domestic violence or an abusive relationship.

Visit pcadv.org for a "Is This Abuse?" quiz.